heavenly bodies

heavenly

published by bbc books,
a division of
bbc enterprises limited
woodlands,
80 wood lane,
london
w12 ott

first published 1994

© iain nicolson 1994
the moral right of the author
has been asserted

isbn 0 563 37033 5

diagrams by line & line

designed by moondisks ltd,
cambridge

printed by cambus litho ltd,
east kilbride
and bound by hunter & foulis ltd,
edinburgh

colour separations by radstock
reproductions ltd,
midsomer norton

to obtain a pack containing a planisphere,
a sundial, a suntracker, a map of the
moon and a chart of the solar system,
send a cheque or postal order for £9.99
payable to bbc education to: bbc
astronomy pack, po box 7, london w3 6xj:
packs available while stocks last

jacket design by bill mason
cover printed by richard clays ltd,
st ives plc

iain nicolson

bodies

contents

introduction

The sky above us is a source of ceaseless fascination and mystery.
Long before the dawn of recorded history humankind must have gazed in
awe and wonder at sights and phenomena beyond human control.

The daytime sky is dominated by the Sun, the source of light and heat
that is essential to sustain life on Earth. With its rising and setting comes day
and night, and the most basic unit of time. The length of the day and the
height to which the Sun rises above the horizon change throughout the year.
This gives the pattern of seasons that is vital to the cycles of planting,
growth, ripening and harvest that sustain agricultural societies. Little
wonder, then, that ancient civilizations regarded the Sun as a powerful god.

The sky at night is studded with stars against which the Moon moves
silently, changing its position and apparent shape night by night as it goes
through its cycle of phases, growing from a thin crescent to 'Full Moon' then
shrinking back to a thin crescent once again. Sometimes the Moon
is high in the sky, sometimes it remains close to the horizon; sometimes
it rises far to the north of east, sometimes well to the south of east.
The Moon provides a pale cold light compared to the Sun, yet its presence
banishes the sometimes frightening blackness of night.

The stars move across the sky from east to west but remain always in
the same patterns, their positions not changing relative to each other.

But which star patterns are visible at night depends on the season of the year; the stars of summer are different from the stars of winter. What controls their comings and goings? Most perplexing of all, perhaps, are the planets, five bright points of light which look like stars yet which wander among them in a puzzling fashion. The naked-eye planets, well-known to the ancients, were named after important deities. To the Romans there was fleet-footed Mercury, the messenger of the Gods, brilliant Venus, the goddess of love, blood-red Mars, the god of war, Jupiter, the king of the gods, and Saturn, the father of Jupiter. Why do they move as they do?

Nowadays, we know that the Sun is a huge globe of incandescent gas, vastly larger than our Earth, that pours huge quantities of light and energy into space. We know that the Earth itself is a planet which, like the other planets, travels round the Sun. The Moon is a smaller globe that travels round the Earth, shining only because it is reflecting some of the sunlight that falls on its surface. We have seen images of the Earth taken from space, men have walked on the Moon and looked back at our planet, hanging in the Moon's sky just as the Moon hangs in ours. Unmanned spacecraft have visited other planets.

Yet, despite all this modern-day knowledge, many of us struggle to understand what we see in the sky, the day-night cycle, the seasons, the motions of Moon and planets, and occasional dramatic phenomena such as eclipses. We puzzle about the links, if any, between the Sun, weather and climate, or between the Moon and the tides

All these movements, phenomena and changes in the sky can be explained by the following facts: the Earth is a globe which spins; the Earth and planets travel round the Sun; the Moon travels round the Earth; and the stars are distant suns. This book, and the television series which it accompanies, tries to make simple sense of these cosmic mysteries. ■

The Sun's dazzling disc brings light and warmth to our planet. Regarded in ancient times as a powerful god, the Sun in fact is our nearest star.

chapter 1

great balls of fire

On a clear dark moonless night, far away from the glare of artificial lights, the sky seems studded with countless stars. With the naked eye, under good conditions, you can see 1500 to 2000 stars on a really good night, but with binoculars vast numbers of fainter stars leap into view.

Some stars appear much brighter than others, but there is one star that is overwhelmingly brighter than all the rest, and far more important. It is much closer to us than any other, and it cannot be seen at night. It is called ... the Sun.

The Sun is the source of light, heat and energy for us here on Earth. Without the Sun, there would be no daylight; its rising and setting brings day and night, our most basic unit of time. Without the Sun, life would never have formed and evolved on Earth, and life could not be sustained. Little wonder, then, that ancient peoples revered the Sun as a powerful god. To the ancient Egyptians, thousands of years ago, the Sun was the god Ra who was born in the morning, carried across the sky in a boat, ferried beneath the Earth, then born again the next morning. To the ancient Greeks, 2500 years ago, the Sun was the god Apollo, riding across the sky in a chariot.

Nowadays, we know that the Sun is a star, a huge globe of incandescent gas, vastly larger than our Earth. With a diameter more than 100 times that of the Earth, its huge globe could contain well over a million bodies the size of our planet. Yet, although the Sun seems large and brilliant to us, it is a very ordinary star. Many stars are bigger and more luminous than our Sun, many others are smaller and less brilliant. The Sun dominates our skies only because it is so much nearer to us than any other star; the nearest star, apart from the Sun itself, is fully a quarter of a million times further away. It is their enormous distances that make stars look like faint points of light. If we lived on a planet revolving round a nearby star, the Sun would be no more than a faint point of light in that planet's sky.

Despite all that astronomers have discovered about our Sun, many of us remain puzzled by its apparent motions in our skies. The Sun rises each morning over the eastern horizon and sets each evening at the western horizon. The stars, too, move across the sky from east to west as the night progresses, but we see different stars in summer than in winter. Why should this be so?

The Spinning Earth

The apparent movements of the Sun and stars, and the seasonal changes in what we see, arise because we view the universe from a moving platform – planet Earth. The Earth spins round on its axis once a day and travels continuously round the Sun along a well-defined path, or orbit. The combination of these motions explains the movements of Sun and stars in the sky.

The Earth spins round from west to east. If you were hovering above the north pole, you would see the Earth turn beneath you in an anticlockwise direction; conversely, if you were poised above the south pole, the Earth would be seen to spin in a clockwise fashion. If you stand on a spinning roundabout, looking outwards from its centre, the rest of the world seems to be whirling around you. You know that it is not, but that is what it looks and feels like. Likewise, because the Earth is spinning from west to east, the Sun and stars appear to move across the sky from east to west. Although we know that the Sun and stars do not revolve round the Earth, it seems as if they do.

The Solar System

The Earth is a planet, a body that travels round the Sun. The Solar System consists of the Sun, the nine planets that revolve round it, and various minor bodies.

The relative sizes of the planetary orbits are shown here, with the orbits of the inner-most three expanded for clarity.

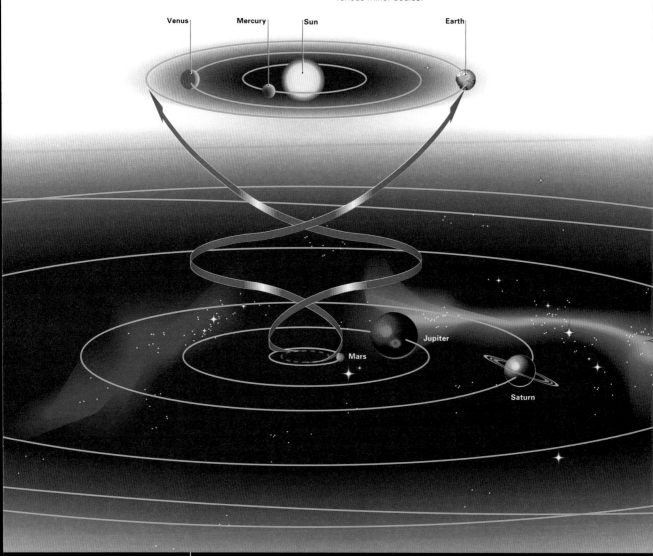

Venus | Mercury | Sun | Earth

Jupiter

Mars

Saturn

The table (right) lists the planets in order of distance from the Sun together with details of their distances and orbital periods. The planets all travel round the Sun in the same direction along paths, or orbits, that lie close to the same plane. Each planet follows an elliptical (oval) orbit but, in most cases, the orbit differs only slightly from a circle. However, the outermost planet, Pluto, follows a markedly elliptical orbit which takes it from just inside the orbit of Neptune out to nearly 50 times the Earth's distance. Because its orbit is tilted to the others by an angle of 17º, it passes above (north of) Neptune's orbit each time it crosses the path of that planet. The relative sizes of the nine planets are shown (below and left) approximately to scale.

Planet	Distance from Sun (Earth's distance = 1)	Distance from Sun (millions of kilometres)	Orbital period (time taken to travel round Sun)
Mercury	0.39	58	88 days
Venus	0.72	108	225 days
Earth	1.00	150	1 year
Mars	1.52	228	1.88 years
Jupiter	5.20	779	11.86 years
Saturn	9.54	1427	29.46 years
Uranus	19.18	2869	84.01 years
Neptune	30.06	4496	164.79 years
Pluto	39.44	5900	247.7 years

Pluto

Uranus

Neptune

Our Moving Planet

The Earth moves round the Sun along a near circular path, or orbit, taking one year to complete each circuit. The Earth is one of nine planets, bodies that travel round the Sun in separate orbits. Five planets are visible to the naked eye, and their existence has been known since the dawn of recorded history. They are Mercury and Venus, that lie closer to the Sun than we do, Mars, Jupiter and Saturn, that lie further out in the depths of space. Three more planets, too faint to be seen with the naked eye, lie further out still: Uranus, Neptune and Pluto. The naked-eye planets look like bright stars but, whereas the stars remain in fixed patterns and do not seem to change their relative positions over a human lifetime, the planets gradually shift position from night to night and month to month. The word 'planet' derives from the Greek *planetes* which means 'wanderer'.

All of the planets move round the Sun in the same direction. Mercury and Venus go round more quickly than the Earth while the other planets, which are further away, go round the Sun more slowly. Mercury takes just 88 days to complete one circuit of the Sun, but distant Pluto takes nearly 248 years. Since a planet's 'year' is equal to the time taken to travel once round its orbit, none of us could expect to survive to a first 'birthday' on Pluto!

The ancient and medieval astronomers firmly believed that the Sun, Moon, stars and planets really did revolve round the Earth once a day. When no one knew the distance and immense size of the Sun, or the nature and vast distances of the stars, it seemed far more logical to assume that all the celestial bodies revolved round the Earth than to imagine that the huge world on which they lived was itself spinning round. To the ancient Greeks, more than 2000 years ago, it seemed as if the stars were fixed to a huge sphere that turned round the Earth once a day.

Although we know that the stars are all individual suns that lie at vast and very different distances from us, when we describe their positions and motions in the sky, it is convenient to imagine that they are fixed to a huge sphere – the celestial sphere – that rotates round the Earth just as the ancient Greeks imagined. By analogy with the Earth, we can define the equator and poles of this sphere. The Earth's axis, extended into space, meets the celestial sphere at the north and south celestial poles; if you were at the north or south pole of the Earth, the north (or south) celestial pole would be vertically overhead. The celestial equator is a circle on the celestial sphere that corresponds to the Earth's equator extended into space; if you were on the Earth's equator, the celestial equator would pass directly overhead. As the Earth turns round, the Sun and stars move across the sky parallel to the celestial equator.

(a)

(b)

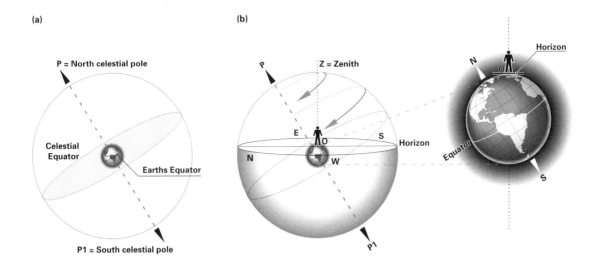

On Earth, the latitude of a place is the angle between the equator and the place, measured north or south from the equator. The latitude of the equator itself is 0°, and the poles are at latitudes 90° north or south. London, England, is at a latitude of about 52°N whereas St Louis, Missouri, is at about 39°N. The equivalent of latitude in the sky is called declination – the angle between the celestial equator and the Sun or a star.

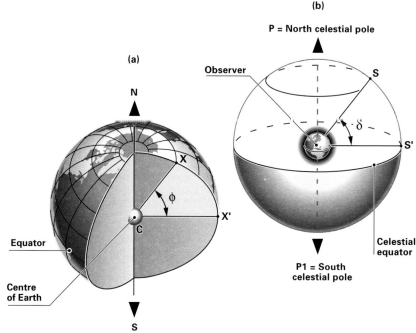

Latitude and declination (above)

a On Earth, the latitude of a place (X) is the angle (φ) between the equator (X'), the Earth's centre (C) and the place (X). Every point on the circle through X, parellel to the equator, has the same latitude.

b The declination (δ) of a star (S) is the angle between the celestial equator (S'), the observer (O) and the star (S).

Ecliptic and Zodiac

The stars that we see in the night-time sky are those which are on the opposite side of the celestial sphere from the Sun. The others are still there, but are drowned out by the dazzling glare of the Sun and the brightness of the daytime sky.

As the Earth moves round the Sun, its 'night' side faces in a progressively-changing direction; for this reason, different stars become visible at different times of the year. To illustrate this, place a lamp on a table, to represent the Sun, and try walking round the table, looking directly away from the 'sun' as you do so. Each time you complete a circuit of the table, you will, in turn, have faced each of the four walls of the room. In a similar way, the constellations visible in the midnight sky will change as the Earth goes round the Sun. The constellation of Leo (the Lion) is well placed around midnight in the spring, the summer sky is dominated by the 'Summer Triangle' comprising the three bright stars, Vega, Deneb and Altair, the autumn sky features Andromeda and Perseus, and the winter sky is dominated by the splendid constellation of Orion.

If we could see the stars in daytime, we would be able to locate the Sun, in the foreground, against the background stars and we would see, from day to day, how its apparent position would change as a result of the Earth's motion around the Sun. In one month, the Earth travels $\frac{1}{12}$ of the way around the Sun and, therefore, moves through an angle of 30° ($\frac{1}{12}$ of a circle) as seen from the Sun. Viewed from the Earth, the Sun appears to shift through an angle of 30° relative to the background stars. In the course of a year, the Earth completes one full circuit around the Sun and, seen from the Earth, the Sun completes one circuit of the celestial sphere relative to the background stars. The path that the Sun traces out relative to the background stars is called the ecliptic. Because the Sun's apparent motion is caused by the motion of the Earth around its orbit, the ecliptic corresponds to the projection of the Earth's orbit onto the celestial sphere.

The Earth's axis is tilted over at an angle of 23·5°; likewise, the Earth's equator is tilted at an angle of 23·5° to the plane of its orbit. The ecliptic is a circle on the celestial sphere that lies in the same plane as the Earth's orbit. The celestial equator, on the other hand, is a circle on the celestial sphere that lies in the plane of the Earth's equator. If the Earth's equator is tilted by 23·5° to its orbit, the ecliptic must be tilted to the celestial equator by this same angle.

The two circles cross at two points, called the vernal ('spring') and autumnal equinoxes, on opposite sides of the sphere. The vernal equinox is the point where the Sun passes from south to north of the celestial equator on or around 21 March each year, and the autumnal equinox is where the Sun passes from north to south of the celestial equator on or around 23 September each year.

The Moon and naked-eye planets are always to be found within an 18°-wide band of sky, centred on the ecliptic, that is known as the zodiac. During the course of a year, the Sun passes through each of the constellations that lie in the zodiac: Aries (the ram), Taurus (the bull), Gemini (the twins), Cancer (the crab), Leo (the lion), Virgo (the virgin), Libra (the scales), Scorpius (the scorpion), Sagittarius (the archer), Capricornus (the goat), Aquarius (the water-carrier) and Pisces (the fish).

At any particular time, the Sun will be 'in' one of these constellations; for example, the Sun is 'in' the constellation of Gemini in June and Cancer in July.

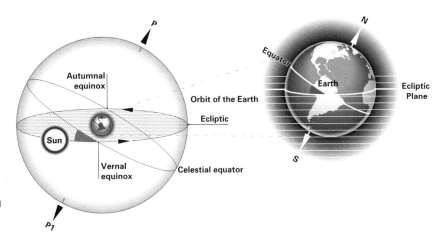

Orbit of the Earth

Ecliptic

Celestial equator

Autumnal equinox

Vernal equinox

Sun

P

P₁

N

Equator

Earth

Ecliptic Plane

S

Tilted ecliptic

The Earth's axis is not perpendicular to the plane of its orbit but instead is tilted at an angle of about 23·5°. The Earth's equator is tilted to the plane of its orbit by this same angle. Because the apparent motion of the Sun along the ecliptic is caused by the Earth's motion around its orbit, the ecliptic is in the same plane as the Earth's orbit. If the Earth's equator is tilted to the plane of its orbit, then the celestial equator and ecliptic must be tilted relative to each other by the same angle. The Sun spends half the year south, and the other half north, of the celestial equator. The points where the ecliptic crosses the celestial equator are the vernal and autumnal equinoxes.

Astrology, the study of patterns of events in the sky and how these might influence affairs of state or lives and personalities of individuals, developed over thousands of years in different ways in different parts of the world. In Western culture, astrological ideas probably originated in the Middle East in Mesopotamia, a region that contained all of what is now Iraq and part of Syria. At first, it was concerned with celestial omens and broad influences. Only rather later, perhaps around the sixth century BC, was the idea of personal horoscopes developed by the Chaldeans, and the Hellenistic Greeks of Alexandria. These ancient astrologers divided up the zodiac into twelve 'signs', each 30° wide ($12 \times 30° = 360°$, a full circle) and, at the time when these ideas were being developed, some 2500 years ago, the 'signs' corresponded to the actual zodiacal constellations. Thus, in those days, the Sun was 'in' Aries in late March and early-to mid-April, moved into Taurus in late April, and so on throughout the year.

In order to 'cast' a horoscope for an individual, an astrologer first of all requires to know the date and place of that person's birth.

The Earth's motion: ecliptic and zodiac

As the Earth moves round the Sun from E1 to E2, the Sun – seen from the Earth – appears to move from S1 to S2 relative to the distant stars. In a year, the Sun appears to travel once around the celestial sphere, along a path called the ecliptic. The band of twelve constellations through which the Sun passes is called the zodiac. The stars which we see at night are those which lie on the opposite side of the Earth from the Sun; different ones come into view as the Earth progresses around its orbit.

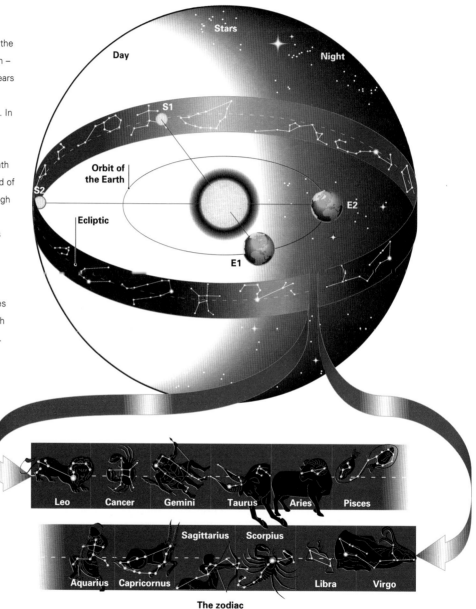

Leo   Cancer   Gemini   Taurus   Aries   Pisces

Aquarius   Capricornus   Sagittarius   Scorpius   Libra   Virgo

The zodiac

The astrologer then works out which sign of the zodiac was rising or culminating (reaching its highest point above the horizon) and plots the positions of the planets at that time. Based on this information, and the supposed characteristics associated with each zodiacal sign and planet, the astrologer then claims to be able to determine the main features of the personality and future of the person concerned.

Modern science can find no rational basis for astrology and rejects its claims. Nevertheless, many people still pay a surprising amount of attention to what their horoscopes have to say – even the 'Your Stars' section in the daily and weekly newspapers which necessarily have to apply equally to the millions upon millions of people who happen to have been born in the same month.

Because of a phenomenon called 'precession' – the apparent slow movement of the celestial poles and the equinoxes – the ancient astrological signs no longer correspond to the constellations of the same names. Think of a spinning top. If you tilt its axis away from the vertical, the axis will itself slowly change direction, tracing out a cone-shape as the top of the axis circles around. The Earth's axis behaves in a similar way, but takes 26,000 years to complete each circuit. During this time, the positions of the north and south celestial poles trace out large circles in the sky. At present, the north celestial pole lies within 1° of a reasonably bright star called Polaris, the Pole Star. In 2500 BC, about the time the great Egyptian pyramids were being constructed, the 'pole star' was Thuban (in the constellation of Draco, the Dragon), while in about 12,000 years' time the north celestial pole will lie close to Vega, the fifth-brightest star in the sky.

This phenomenon also causes the positions of the equinoxes to shift slowly westwards on the celestial sphere. The vernal equinox, the point where the Sun crosses the celestial equator in the spring each year, makes one complete circuit around the celestial sphere in 26,000 years and moves through an angle of about 30° every 2000 years or so. For this reason, the position of the vernal equinox shifts from one zodiacal constellation to the next every 2000 years or so and, having passed through all twelve of the zodiacal constellations, returns to its original position after 26,000 years.

Two thousand years ago, the vernal equinox was in the constellation of Aries (for this reason, it is also known as the 'First Point of Aries') and the Sun entered that constellation around 21 March each year. Nowadays, thanks to precession, the vernal equinox lies in the constellation of Pisces, and the Sun is in that constellation on 21 March; in the near future, precession will carry the vernal equinox into the next zodiacal constellation, Aquarius. During the last two millennia, the old astrological signs have slipped round by one complete sign compared to the actual constellations of the same name. If your 'star sign' is Aries (21 March to 20 April), the Sun is actually in Pisces on your birthday.

Daytime Star

The Sun itself is the one star that can be studied in detail. All the other stars are so far away that, even when seen through the largest telescopes, they still look just like points of light; the telescope makes them much brighter, but does not enlarge them sufficiently to show them as round discs like our Sun. Because it is big, bright, and around in daytime, the Sun is an ideal subject for amateur observation.

However, the following warning is vital: NEVER look directly at the Sun through a telescope or binoculars; the concentrated heat and light will cause severe and permanent eye damage in an instant, and almost certainly will cause permanent blindness. Do not gaze directly at the Sun even with the naked eye.

The safe way to observe the Sun is by projection. Place a screen – a white sheet of paper or card will do – behind the eyepiece end of the telescope and look at the shadow of the telescope on the screen. Do not look along (or through!) the telescope at the Sun. Move the telescope around until its shadow is circular; the Sun's light should then be passing straight through the telescope and out of its eyepiece, and an image of the Sun should be falling on the screen. If not, a slight movement of the telescope should be enough to bring the Sun's image into view. Slide the eyepiece in and out until you have a sharply-focused image. It is a good idea to have a piece of card handy, with a hole in the centre, that can be slid over the telescope tube to cast a shadow and prevent direct sunlight (which has not passed through the telescope) from flooding the screen.

The Sun can then be viewed in safety, and its image on the screen sketched or photographed. Because the Sun is so bright, very short exposures will suffice. If your camera has a 'through the lens' light meter, that will tell you what exposure to use, but it is always wise to take several additional exposures, shorter and longer than the indicated value. Unless the telescope is driven by a motor to track the motion of the Sun across the sky, the Sun's image will drift across the screen and will disappear from view after a couple of minutes. However, it is easy to centre up the image again by hand, and simple 'point and click' photographs will not be blurred by this motion because the exposures are so short that the Sun's moving image is 'frozen'. This drifting of the Sun's image is a marvellous demonstration of the Earth's rotation.

Small dark spots and more complex groups of spots will often be seen on the Sun's disc. If you are concerned that they might be due to bits of dust on your eyepiece, move the telescope slightly; the genuine spots will move with the image of the Sun. These dark spots and patches are known, not surprisingly, as 'sunspots'. They are regions of the solar surface that are cooler than their surroundings. The visible surface of the Sun, which is called the 'photosphere' (literally, 'sphere of light'), has a temperature of nearly 6000° Celsius. The central part of a typical sunspot is about 2000° cooler at a mere 4000° Celsius! Because sunspots are cooler, they give out less light than the adjacent photosphere and so appear dark by contrast with their much more brilliant surroundings. Sunspots are areas of concentrated magnetism up to 10,000 times as powerful as the magnetic field which causes compass needles to line up in a north-south direction at the surface of the Earth. They range in size from tiny spots at the limit of visibility to huge groups covering billions of square kilometres. Sunspots were first recorded telescopically in the early part of the seventeenth century. There is some dispute as to who first achieved this, but credit is usually given to the great Italian astronomer Galileo Galilei. From time to time, a spot, or spot group, is sufficiently large to be seen with the naked eye when the Sun is heavily dimmed by haze or mist (again, beware: do not stare at the Sun with the naked eye), and sightings of naked-eye sunspots can be traced back as far as 800 BC in the records of Chinese observers.

Sunspots

This view of the Sun's disc shows a number of large dark sunspots. The picture was taken on 18 August 1989, a few months before the maximum in the 11-year cycle of solar activity.

Solar prominence (right)

This flame-like solar prominence has surged to a height of 330,000 kilometres above the Sun's surface.

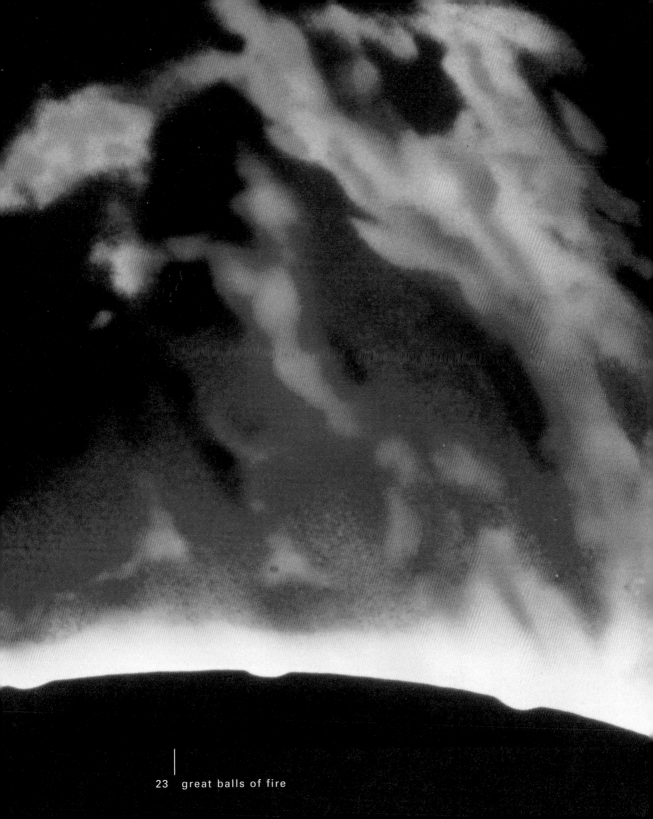

great balls of fire

Many observatories around the world used to make daily records, whenever conditions permitted, of the numbers and positions of sunspots. Only a few professional observatories keep sunspot records today, but amateur observers still play an important role in keeping track of these intriguing phenomena. Anyone can do it, with very modest equipment.

Observations of sunspots show that the Sun rotates on its axis. If a particular spot is plotted, day by day, its position will be seen to shift across the visible disc. Eventually, the spot will disappear around the edge of the Sun and then, if the spot lasts long enough, it will reappear at the opposite side of the disc about two weeks later. Some spots last long enough to be seen on more than one rotation (the record lifetime for a spot is believed to be about 200 days), but most last for only a few days or a few weeks.

Galileo, from his observations, begun in 1610, showed that the Sun turns round in a period of about a month. Later observations revealed that the Sun does not rotate like a solid body; the rotation period close to the equator is about 25 days, but further from the equator, the period is longer; for example, at 30° north or south of the solar equator, the period is about 27 days and, close to the poles, some 34 days.

Long-term records show that the number of sunspots increases and decreases in a fairly regular cycle, reaching a maximum, on average, once every 11 years. The sunspot cycle was identified in 1843, following a long series of observations by the German amateur astronomer, Heinrich Schwabe. At a sunspot maximum, the solar disc is heavily spotted, but at a minimum, the Sun's face may be spotless for weeks on end.

In 1890, from an investigation of old records, the English astronomer E. W. Maunder showed that between 1645 and 1715, there seemed to have been virtually no spots at all. This gap in the cycle, now known as the

Maunder Minimum, coincided with a prolonged period of exceptionally cold winters in Europe. In the middle part of this period, known as the 'little ice age', the river Thames, in London, regularly froze over so thickly that 'frost fairs', where tents and stalls were erected and bonfires lit were held on its icy surface. More tenuous evidence suggests that during the past few thousand years there have been other prolonged periods of depressed solar activity that have coincided with spells of colder-than-average climate. There seems to be a link between long-term changes in solar activity and weather and climate here on Earth but, as yet, we do not understand exactly how the connection works.

Sunspots are one symptom of the underlying solar cycle which is related to changes in the way magnetic forces are concentrated in and above the solar surface. Other kinds of activity include prominences – flame-like clouds of glowing gas that surge up and down from the Sun's surface, or which may hang for weeks or months suspended in the solar atmosphere – and flares – violent releases of energy that erupt from time to time, usually in the vicinity of a complex sunspot group. A major flare can emit within about 20 minutes or so as much energy as several billion one-megaton hydrogen bombs; this energy leaves the Sun in various forms – visible light, x-rays, radio waves and high-speed atomic particles, some of which travel at large fractions of the speed of light. Radiation from a solar flare affects the upper atmosphere and can disrupt radio communication. The blast of atomic particles causes magnetic disturbances here on Earth, creating surges in electrical power cables that are occasionally are strong enough to blow transformers, and produces glowing patterns of shifting light in the polar skies that are known as the aurora borealis (northern lights) and aurora australis (southern lights).

Seeing for Yourself

Anyone, with a modest telescope or even binoculars, can make records of the numbers and locations of sunspots. By keeping records over a matter of weeks, you can see for yourself the rate at which the Sun spins on its axis, and by keeping records over years or decades, the increase and decrease of the sunspot numbers will be revealed. If you do become interested in this kind of work, it makes sense to collaborate with others who are doing the same kind of thing by joining your local astronomical society or a national society such as, in Britain, the British Astronomical Association, or the Society for Popular Astronomy, both of which have solar sections that specialize in what amateurs can contribute to the study of our daytime star.

If you do not have a telescope, you can still project a solar image with the aid of a pinhole camera. In essence, this is simply a box with a screen (a piece of white paper will do) at one end and a small circular hole (made by a pin or drilled out with a fine drill bit) through which sunlight can pass at the other. Sunlight will form a small image of the Sun on the screen, and the greater the separation between pinhole and screen, the larger the image (a 1-metre (3-foot) distance will give a solar image about 1 centimetre ($\frac{1}{2}$ inch) across). Try different sized holes and differing separations to see which gives the best image. Once you have found the image, leave the box where it is, and you will soon see the effect of the Earth's rotation carry the solar disc across the screen. If a solar eclipse occurs (where the Moon passes partly or completely in front of the Sun), then the pinhole camera will show this too.

standing stones and sun gazers

Throughout north-western Europe from Brittany to the Shetlands, but particularly in the British Isles, there are hundreds of mysterious arrangements of standing stones, ranging from isolated single stones or pairs of stones to complex circles containing dozens of stones.

Stonehenge, in Wiltshire, is by far the best-known of these structures. Seventeen standing stones, some of them linked by massive lintels, remain of the 30 which originally formed the main circle. Five pairs of even larger stones, each weighing up to 50 tonnes, lie inside the main circle and there are several outlying stones, too. Stonehenge is a complex structure that was built, modified and reconstructed in several stages over a period of about 1000 years starting in about 2800 BC. Debate about why and how this intriguing structure was constructed has raged for centuries. Was it a form of astronomical computer, did its purpose relate to keeping track of the seasons or predicting eclipses, was it a religious or ceremonial centre, or was its function even more mystical and mysterious? It retains a powerful grip on the human imagination today, from academics to New Age travellers, and is one of the key tourist attractions in south-west England.

Elaborate and imposing though it may be, Stonehenge is only one among hundreds of structures erected by the megalithic people of north-western Europe between about 3500 and 1500 BC. Elaborate circles exist elsewhere, too, for example at Callanish in the Isle of Lewis, at Stenness in Orkney and at Avebury in Wiltshire. Less imposing, but nevertheless intriguing, structures exist in abundance. One is at Swinside, in the Cumbrian fells of north-west England, where about 40 modest stones are arranged in a circle nearly 30 metres (100 feet) across with an 'entrance' facing south-east, towards the direction of the rising Sun in midwinter. When this circle was built, some 4000 years ago, the stone-age people who lived in the area would have been farmers, dependent for their livelihood on planting, tending and reaping their crops in tune with the seasons.

It seems likely that at least one reason for the building of stone circles was to monitor the rising and setting positions of the Sun in order to keep track of the seasons as they progressed from the long days and short nights of summer to the short days and long dreary nights of winter.

The Seasons

At any instant, half of the Earth's globe is lit up by the Sun and the other half is in darkness. As the Earth spins round, the place where you live is carried round from darkness into sunlight and from daylight back into night in an endless cycle. Sunrise occurs when you cross the boundary between shadow and light, noon occurs when you cross the centre-line of the sunlit side and sunset occurs when you are carried back into shadow.

If the Earth's axis were perpendicular to the plane of its orbit, the Sun would always be overhead at the equator; if you lived at the equator, the Sun would pass directly overhead at noon every day of the year. If you were at the north or south pole, the Sun would always be visible, right down on the horizon, and there would be no day or night. The boundary between day and night would run from pole to pole and every part of the Earth's surface, apart from the poles themselves, would experience equal periods of light and dark; day and night would be of equal length everywhere on the Earth's surface. The Sun would rise precisely due east and set precisely due west wherever you were (apart from at the poles themselves). There would be no seasons. Every day would be exactly the same with 12 hours of daylight and 12 hours of night.

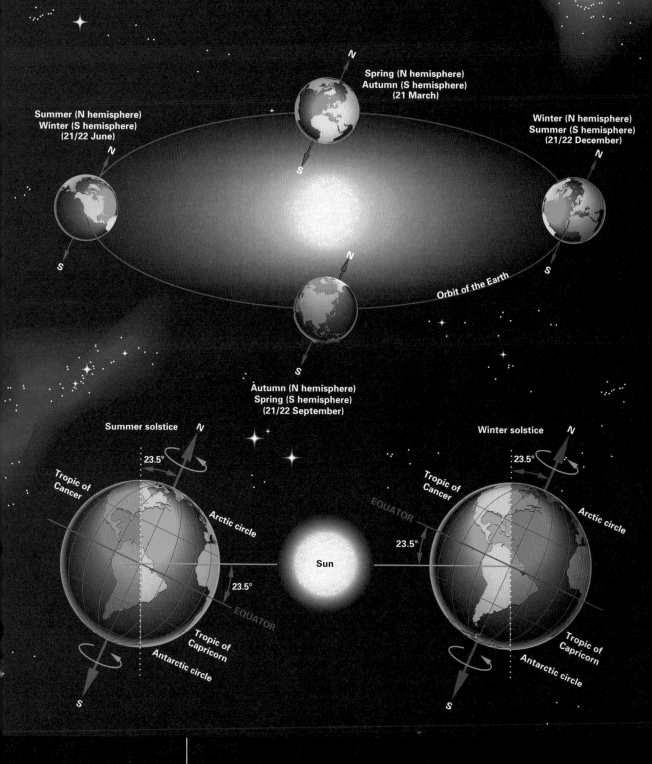

Spring (N hemisphere)
Autumn (S hemisphere)
(21 March)

Summer (N hemisphere)
Winter (S hemisphere)
(21/22 June)

Winter (N hemisphere)
Summer (S hemisphere)
(21/22 December)

Orbit of the Earth

Autumn (N hemisphere)
Spring (S hemisphere)
(21/22 September)

Summer solstice

23.5°

Tropic of
Cancer

Arctic circle

23.5°

EQUATOR

Tropic of
Capricorn

Antarctic circle

Sun

Winter solstice

23.5°

Tropic of
Cancer

Arctic circle

EQUATOR

23.5°

Tropic of
Capricorn

Antarctic circle

The seasons (left)

Because of the tilt of the Earth's axis, in late December the Sun is overhead at the tropic of Capricorn and everywhere in the southern hemisphere experiences more than 12 hours of daylight per day. Six months later, when the Earth is on the opposite side of the Sun, the Sun is vertically overhead at the tropic of Cancer and everywhere in the northern hemisphere has more than 12 hours of daylight per day.

The midnight Sun (below)

Within the Arctic circle during the height of summer, the Sun does not set but instead remains above the horizon at all times, giving continuous daylight for 24 hours a day. As shown here, the Sun reaches its lowest altitude when it passes due north and then begins to climb again. Six months later the Arctic circle will be in darkness and the midnight Sun will be seen from the Antarctic.

In fact, the Earth's axis is tilted at an angle of 23·5°. Apart from the slow change caused by precession, as mentioned in Chapter 1, the Earth's axis points in a constant direction in space. When the Earth is one side of the Sun (December), the south pole is lit up for 24 hours a day and the north pole is in darkness for 24 hours a day; 6 months later (June), by which time the Earth has moved round to the opposite side of the Sun, the south pole is in darkness and the north pole experiences continuous sunlight.

So far as the northern hemisphere is concerned, midwinter occurs on or around 22 December each year. On that date, everywhere within 23·5° of the north pole, inside the Arctic circle, is in complete darkness and experiences no daylight at all because, as the Earth turns round, the Sun remains always below the horizon. At noon, the Sun passes vertically overhead at places along the Tropic of Capricorn, a circle round the globe at latitude 23·5°S. Everywhere within 23·5° of the south pole, inside the Antarctic circle, experiences permanent daylight.

Three months later, after the Earth has moved one quarter of the way around its orbit, the Sun is overhead at the equator and rays of sunlight graze the Earth's surface at each pole. The boundary between sunlight and shadow extends from pole to pole and day and night are of equal duration everywhere on the Earth's surface. This date, which falls on or around 21 March each year, is known as the spring, or 'vernal', equinox (from 'equi', equal; and 'nox', night) and marks the official beginning of spring in the northern hemisphere; and autumn in the southern.

After a further 3 months, on or around 21 June each year, the Earth has completed half its journey round the Sun, and everywhere within the Arctic circle remains bathed in sunlight for 24 hours a day while everywhere in the Antarctic circle is in darkness. The Sun is overhead at noon at places lying along a circle at latitude 23·5°N (the Tropic of Cancer), and it is midsummer's day in the northern hemisphere.

By September the Earth has completed three-quarters of its orbit, the Sun once again is overhead at the equator, and day and night are again of equal duration everywhere on the planet. This date, on or around 23 September, is the autumnal equinox and marks the beginning of autumn in the northern hemisphere. Finally, on 22 December, the Earth completes its 940 million kilometre (584 million mile) journey around the Sun and it is midwinter again.

High Sun and Low Sun

The duration of daylight and the height of the Sun above the horizon at noon are both affected by these seasonal changes, the difference in day length being greatest near the poles and least near the equator. At the equator itself, night and day are always of equal duration.

At either equinox, the noon Sun is vertically overhead at the equator, and is on the horizon at the north and south poles. The noon altitude at other places lies between these extremes; the higher the latitude, the lower the altitude. For example, in London (latitude 51·5°N), the noon altitude of the Sun is 38·5°, while in St Louis, Missouri (38·7° N), it is 51·3°.

At the summer solstice, when the Sun is overhead at the Tropic of Cancer, the Sun has moved along the ecliptic to a point (also called the summer solstice) where it is 23·5° north of the celestial equator. Its noon altitude is then 23·5° greater than it was at the vernal equinox – 62° when seen from London and 74·8° when viewed from St Louis.

The Sun and the seasons (right)

At an equinox, the Sun is vertically overhead at the equator and so, seen from the Earth, lies precisely on the celestial equator. It then rises due east and sets due west. At the summer solstice, the Sun is overhead at the tropic of Cancer and moves across the sky on a track 23·5° north of the celestial equator, the greater part of which is above the horizon. Six months later, the Sun is 23·5° south of the celestial equator and spends less than half of each day above the horizon.

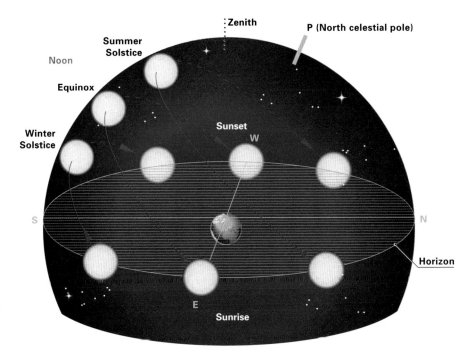

Zenith

P (North celestial pole)

Noon

Summer Solstice

Equinox

Winter Solstice

Sunset

W

S

N

Horizon

E

Sunrise

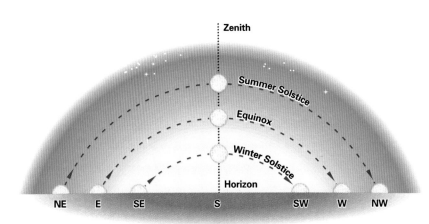

Zenith

Summer Solstice

Equinox

Winter Solstice

Horizon

NE   E   SE   S   SW   W   NW

High Sun – low Sun (left)

At an equinox, the Sun rises due east and sets due west. At the summer solstice, the Sun rises north of east, reaches a noon altitude 23·5° higher than on an equinox, and sets north of west. At the winter solstice it rises south of east, reaches a noon altitude 23·5° lower than on an equinox and sets south of west.

By contrast, at the winter solstice, the Sun is 23·5° south of the celestial equator and its noon altitude is 23·5° less than it was at the vernal equinox – 15° in London and 27·8° in St Louis. The midwinter Sun in Great Britain seems to crawl reluctantly over the horizon, and stays low down, dazzling motorists' eyes on the days when it deigns to peep out from behind the clouds.

Long Days and Short Days

The celestial equator crosses the horizon at two points – due east and due west. At the equinoxes, when the Sun is on the celestial equator, it rises due east and sets due west and spends equal amounts of time above and below the horizon. At other times of the year, when it is north or south of the equator, the Sun moves across the sky parallel to the celestial equator, tracing out a circle centred on the north or the south celestial pole.

Because the Sun's declination shifts between 23·5°N and 23·5°S, the duration of daylight, and the positions of its rising and setting points, vary with the seasons. After the spring equinox, the Sun moves, day by day, progressively further to the north of the celestial equator and so rises to the north of east and sets to the north of west. It spends more time above the horizon than below, because the greater part of its circle round the pole is above the horizon. The rising and setting points advance further towards the north until the summer solstice ('solstice' means 'standstill of the Sun') – midsummer's day – when it rises as far to the north of east and sets as far to the north of west as it can do. This is the 'longest day'. For a few days around this date, there is little change in the rising and setting points.

Thereafter, the rising point returns towards the east and the setting point returns towards the west, reaching due east and due west again at the autumnal equinox. From then on, the Sun moves progressively south of the celestial equator and, as the weeks go by, it rises progressively further to the south of east and sets ever further south of west. It spends less and less time above the horizon, the duration of daylight decreases and the nights become longer until, at the winter solstice, the day is shortest and the night is longest. From then on, the Sun begins to move back towards the celestial equator; the duration of daylight increases and the nights shorten until, at the next spring equinox, they are equal again and the Sun once more rises due east and sets due west.

The changes in rising and setting positions become more extreme as you approach closer to the poles. On midsummer's day at latitude 52°N, the Sun rises 40° north of east, sets 40° north of west and remains above the horizon for 16·7 hours. On midwinter's day, it rises 40° south of east and sets 40° south of west, spending just 7·5 hours above the horizon. In Edinburgh (latitude 56°N) the day length ranges from 17·6 hours to 7 hours while at Stenness, in the Orkney islands (latitude 59°N), the Sun remains above the horizon for 18·5 hours on midsummer's day and the sky does not really become dark at all; in midwinter, however, the day lasts for just 6 hours. Further north than 66·5°, the Sun does not set at all in the middle of summer and does not rise at all in the middle of winter.

You can see these effects for yourself by making simple observations throughout the year. If you are an early riser, try standing in the same position at each sunrise and note where the Sun is rising relative to distant objects such as trees, buildings, or whatever is available. If you are not too keen on getting up early, try making these observations at sunset instead!

By making these observations, you will probably have been doing something similar to what the megalithic builders of stone circles were doing thousands of years ago. There is ongoing disagreement among archaeo-astronomers (astronomers who study ancient stone alignments) and archaeologists as to whether or not ancient stone circles had astronomical functions. Some have argued that with a circle containing many stones, there are so many possible sighting lines that almost any alignment could be claimed. For example, in a 12-stone circle, 11 alignments can be made between the first stone and the rest, a further 10 between the remaining 10, and so on, giving 66 in all. Since it is possible to look either way along each line, this number has to be doubled. Nevertheless, there seems little doubt that at least some of them were set up to align with the rising and setting points of the Sun at the equinoxes or the solstices to keep track of the seasons and perhaps, in some cases, to enable the astronomer-priests to predict the most mysterious and dramatic of events – eclipses.

How Long Is a Day?

The length of a day may be defined as the time interval between two successive noons, two successive occasions when the Sun reaches the meridian and is at its highest point above the horizon. This time interval is called the solar day, or, to be more precise, the apparent solar day, and is divided into 24 hours of (apparent) solar time. On this basis, we have 24 hours of equal length and more hours of daylight in summer than in winter. It was not always so; the Babylonians and ancient Egyptians, 4000 years ago, simply divided daytime into 12 'hours', and had longer 'hours' in summer than in winter.

Sundials

Apparent solar time is what is indicated by sundials. A sundial is basically a development of the shadow stick. As the Sun moves across the sky, the shadow cast by a vertical stick also moves around, and changes in length as the Sun rises higher or sinks lower in the sky. The shadow is shortest at noon, when the Sun is highest and is longest at sunrise and sunset.

The Earth turns through an angle of 15° every hour (360° in 24 hours) and the Sun moves across the sky at the same rate. However, the shadow cast on a horizontal surface moves at a variable rate because the Sun is

The Sundial

A sundial usually consists of a horizontal or vertical plate and a rod, or 'style' which casts a shadow onto the plate. The style is tilted at an angle which depends on the latitude of the site. As the Sun moves across the sky, the shadow of the style sweeps across the plate and the edge of the shadow indicates the time. The vertical sundial shown here is located on East Bergholt Church, Suffolk. The shadow indicates about 11.10 am, solar time.

moving in a plane that is tilted to the horizontal. Try setting up a shadow stick (check that it is vertical by using a plumb bob – a weight suspended on a string) and sticking pegs in the ground to mark the position of the shadow at hourly intervals; this will show how the length of the shadow and the angle between successive hours varies throughout the day.

A sundial usually consists of a horizontal or vertical plate on which the hours and divisions of hours are marked and a rod or triangle, called the style, which casts a shadow onto the plate. The style is set up along the north-south direction with the edge that casts the shadow pointing towards the north celestial pole; the edge is then parallel to the Earth's axis, the axis around which the Sun seems to move in its daily motion across the sky. Because the plate is horizontal, the angles between the hour lines will not be equal. Most garden sundials are of this type.

Star Time

We can also define the length of a day as the time interval between two successive occasions on which a particular star crosses the observer's meridian and, if we do this, we find that there is a small but significant difference between the length of the sidereal day (the day measured by the apparent motion of the stars) and the apparent solar day. The difference is caused by the Earth's motion round the Sun.

The true rotation period of the Earth is the time it takes to turn once round its axis relative to the background of distant stars. A star that is due south in the sky, on the meridian, is said to be at 'upper transit'. If you face south, you will be looking out into space, directly towards that star. After one complete rotation of the Earth you will, once again, be facing directly

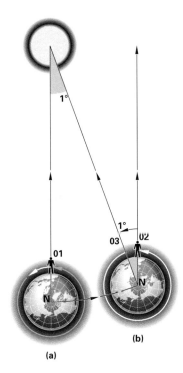

(b)

(a)

Day length

At noon **a**, the observer at O1 is looking directly towards the Sun. After one complete rotation of the Earth **b**, the observer is at position O2. Because the Earth has moved a little way round the Sun, the Earth will have to rotate a little further, to O3, before the next noon occurs.

towards that star, and it will have returned to upper transit. The name given to the time interval between two successive upper transits of a star is called the sidereal day.

If the Earth were stationary, the Sun would return to the meridian, and noon would occur, at intervals precisely equal to the rotation period of the Earth; the solar day and sidereal day would be equal. But the Earth is moving and travels along its orbit through an angle of about 1° (as seen from the Sun) per day. Before the Sun can return to an observer's meridian, the Earth must turn through 360° (one complete rotation) plus the extra degree; between two successive noons it turns through 361° rather than 360°. The Earth takes about 4 minutes to turn through an angle of 1° and so the solar day is about 4 minutes longer than the sidereal day.

In a year, the Sun rises and sets 365 times, there are 365 noons and 365 solar days. However, the Earth actually spins round on its axis 366 times, and any particular star rises, culminates and sets 366 times a year. A year contains 366 sidereal days. In effect, the 4-minute difference in day length adds up over a year to one whole day, and one rising and setting of the Sun is 'cancelled out' by the motion of the Earth round the Sun.

Everyday clocks and calendars are based on solar time because it is the rising and setting of the Sun that regulates our lives, not the rising and setting of the stars. However, the difference in day length causes any particular star to cross the meridian 4 minutes earlier each successive night, and 2 hours earlier each successive month. If Sirius, the brightest star in the sky, is due south at midnight at the beginning of January, it will be due south at 2200 hours (10.00 pm) at the beginning of February, and will be invisible six months later (in July) because it will then be due south at midday and will be lost in the glare of the daylight sky.

Unequal Days

The time intervals between successive noons are not precisely equal, and solar days, therefore, are not all identical in length. There are two reasons for this rather perplexing state of affairs, one relating to the shape of the Earth's orbit and the other to the tilt of the ecliptic.

Firstly, the Earth's orbit is an ellipse (an oval path), not a circle and so, as the Earth moves round the Sun, its distance from the Sun varies between 147 million kilometres (91 million miles) and 152 million kilometres (94 million miles). The speed at which the Earth moves also varies, being slowest when furthest away and fastest when closest in.

Because the Earth's speed around the Sun varies, the rate at which the Sun appears to move relative to the background stars also varies. This affects the instant at which the Sun crosses the meridian on successive days and so makes a difference to the time at which noon occurs when compared with a clock that keeps uniform time.

The time interval between successive noons is affected by the rate at which the Sun is moving eastwards parallel to the celestial equator. Because the ecliptic is tilted, the Sun's motion is partly eastwards (parallel to the celestial equator) and partly north-south (perpendicular to the equator). Near the equinoxes, the Sun is moving rapidly north or south and the eastwards component of its motion is least, while near the summer and winter solstices, the north-south part of its motion is least and the easterly part greatest. This also affects the time interval between successive transits and so affects the length of the solar day.

Because of these effects, apparent (sundial) time deviates from a uniform time rate by up to 16 minutes. In centuries gone by, this difference would not have mattered, but as clocks became more accurate, and life came to rely more and more on precise timetables, the variation in apparent time became more and more inconvenient. A uniform time system called mean time was introduced. This system divides up the year into $365\frac{1}{4}$ mean solar days each of precisely equal length, and each containing 24 identical hours of mean time. Greenwich Mean Time (mean time measured at the Royal Observatory, Greenwich) became the standard time system for England in 1880.

The difference between apparent solar time and mean time is called the equation of time. The two times coincide on four dates in the year (16 April, 15 June, 2 September and 26 December). Apparent (sundial) time is ahead of mean time between 16 April and 15 June and again between 2 September and 26 December, being furthest ahead (16·3 minutes) on 4 November; apparent time lags behind mean time for the rest of the year, being furthest behind (14 minutes) on 11 February.

To convert sundial time to mean time, subtract the value of the equation of time from sundial time when apparent time is ahead of mean time, and add the value of the equation of time to sundial time when apparent time is behind mean time. For example, on 4 November, apparent time is 16 minutes ahead of mean time. When your sundial reads 1200 hours (noon) the mean time will be 1200 − 16 minutes = 1144. On 11 February, when apparent time is 14 minutes behind mean time, 1200 hours on your sundial will correspond to 1200 + 14 minutes = 1214 hours mean time.

Do not attempt to catch a train, bus or plane by sundial time unless you correct for the equation of time. But when precise time is not required, why not stay in tune with nature, and stick with sundial time?

The crescent Moon is seen here over the jagged slopes of Mt Blanc. Its changing shape, or phase, has intrigued sky-watchers since the dawn of human history.

chapter

3

blue moon

Down the ages, the Moon has exerted a powerful grip on our imaginations. At night, it casts a cold, silvery light. It seems to move in mysterious ways. Sometimes it sets soon after the Sun, sometimes we can see it all night long, at other times it does not rise until just before sunrise. For a few nights each month it cannot be seen at all. It changes shape, night by night. Sometimes it stays low down, on other nights it is high in the sky. Most ancient civilizations revered the mysterious Moon as a goddess.

The Moon is our nearest neighbour in space, and the only world – apart from the Earth – on which humankind has trod. Just over a quarter of the Earth's size, it lies at a distance of some 384,000 kilometres (238,000 miles), a distance equivalent to about 30 times the Earth's diameter – 30 bodies the size of the Earth laid in a row would stretch from here to the Moon. Because it travels round the Earth in an elliptical orbit, its distance varies from 356,400 kilometres (221,000 miles) to 406,000 kilometres (252,000 miles).

Because the Moon travels round the Earth it spends some time in the daytime sky as well as in the night sky. The Moon is very faint indeed compared to the Sun but, nevertheless, it is surprising how often, if you look carefully, you can see the faint Moon against a clear blue daytime sky, especially in the morning or late afternoon.

Waxing Moon – Waning Moon

The Moon changes its apparent shape, or phase, night by night, growing from a thin crescent, visible in the early evening sky, to a fully-illuminated disc ('Full Moon') that shines throughout the night, then shrinking to a thin crescent, visible just before dawn. After vanishing for a few days,

Blue Moon

The Moon can take on a bluish colour if its light passes through a layer of very tiny dust or ice particles, of just the right size, suspended in the Earth's atmosphere. Suitable conditions occasionally occur after a major forest fire or volcanic eruption. The rarity of the phenomenon has led to the use of the phrase, 'once in a blue Moon' to mean, 'a very rare event'.

it appears again as a thin crescent in the evening sky. The cycle repeats itself at intervals of about a month. The word 'month' was originally derived from the time taken by the Moon to pass through a complete cycle of phases, but the lengths of the calendar months have been adjusted to fit in with a 12-month year.

The Moon has no light of its own; it shines because it reflects sunlight. However, the Sun only illuminates half of the Moon's globe at a time, the other half being in shadow. As the Moon moves round the Earth, the angle between the Sun, Earth and Moon changes, so allowing us to see differing amounts of its sunlit hemisphere.

It is easy to see what is happening with the aid of a white ball on a bright sunny day. Half of the ball will be lit up by the Sun and the other half will be in shadow. Hold the ball at arm's length close to the direction of the Sun in the sky.

**(Remember – never gaze directly at the Sun,
even with the naked eye.)**

Most of it will be in shadow and only a thin crescent will be brightly illuminated. Move it round until you are looking at right angles to the Sun's direction. Now you will see half of the sunlit side and half of the shaded side. Continue to move the ball round and the phase will increase until, when it is held in the opposite direction to the Sun (keep it away from your own shadow), the visible face of the ball will be fully illuminated. If you continue to move the ball round, it will approach closer to the direction of the Sun and less and less of its visible side will be lit up; the 'phase' will shrink to a thin crescent when the ball approaches close to the direction of the Sun.

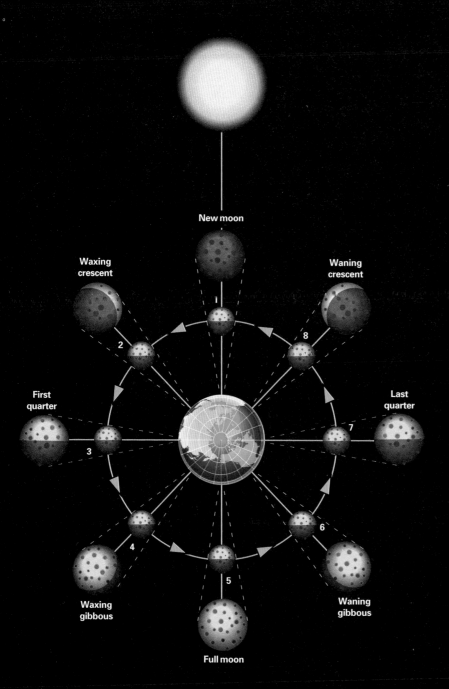

New moon

Waxing
crescent

Waning
crescent

First
quarter

Last
quarter

Waxing
gibbous

Waning
gibbous

Full moon

Phases of the Moon (left)
At any instant, half of the
Moon's surface is lit up by
the Sun and the other half
is in darkness. At New
Moon (1), its Earth-facing
side is dark. As the Moon
continues along its orbit
we see a thin crescent (2)
which grows to a half-illuminated disc (3) – 'first
quarter'. From (4) the phase
grows until Full Moon (5),
which occurs when the
Moon is on the opposite
side of the Earth from the
Sun. Thereafter, the phase
decreases (6), (7), (8)
towards New Moon (1) again.

Earthrise (opposite)
The Earth hangs above the
lunar horizon in this vista
seen from the Apollo 11
spacecraft while it was in
orbit round the Moon in
July 1969. Seen from the
Moon, the Earth passes
through a cycle of phases
from 'New' to 'Full' just as
the Moon does in our
sky. The colourful Earth
contrasts sharply with the
bleakness of the Moon.

(The same demonstration described on page 45 can be done in the dark using a torch beam to represent the Sun.)

The Moon is just another ball, admittedly much larger and much further away, that moves around us, and it shows phases for exactly the same reasons. If the Moon is visible in the daytime sky, try holding the ball in the same direction as the Moon; it will show the same phase.

At 'New Moon', the Sun and Moon are close together in the sky, and the Earth-facing side is in darkness. Usually, at these times, the Moon is actually a little above or a little below the Sun in the sky; if the Moon passes directly between the Sun and the Earth, it hides all or part of the Sun, causing a solar eclipse. Thereafter, the Moon moves steadily to the east of the Sun at a rate of about 12° per day. Its phase increases from a thin crescent to a half-illuminated disc in just over a week. This phase, often called 'half moon', is also known as 'first quarter' as it occurs when the Moon has travelled one quarter of the way round the Earth.

The phase then becomes 'gibbous' ('greater than half') and grows to a fully-illuminated disc ('Full Moon') after a further week or so. Thereafter, as the Moon continues along its orbit around the Earth, it approaches closer to the Sun in the sky and its phase shrinks, reaching last quarter ('half moon' again) about a week after Full and then shrinking to a thin crescent and returning to 'New Moon' after another week or so.

When the phase is growing, the Moon is said to be 'waxing' and when it is shrinking, the Moon is said to be 'waning'. The waxing crescent Moon is visible in the evening sky after sunset, and sets soon after the Sun. As the phase grows, the Moon sets progressively later. At first quarter, it rises around midday and sets around midnight while at 'Full Moon', when the

Sun and Moon are in opposite directions in the sky, the Moon rises in the east around the time when the Sun is setting in the west and remains visible thoughout most or all of the night. By last quarter, it rises about midnight and sets about midday, and by the time it has shrunk to a thin crescent, it is rising just before dawn.

The Face of the Moon

Because the Moon takes precisely the same amount of time to spin on its axis as it does to travel round the Earth, it keeps the same face turned towards us all the time. The far side, likewise, is permanently turned away from Earth. To convince yourself of this, try the following experiment. Place a chair in the centre of a room, to represent the Earth. Now, walk round the chair, facing towards it all the time. After one complete circuit you will have faced, in turn, all four walls of the room, just as you would do if you stayed in one place and turned once around. In going once round the chair, you have also had to rotate once on your axis in order to keep facing the chair at all times. Someone sitting in the chair (a swivel chair is ideal for this) would have seen your face at all times and would never have seen the back of your head. The same applies to the Moon.

If you use a lamp on one wall or in one corner of the room to represent the Sun then, as you move round the chair, you will alternately face towards and away from the lamp and its light will fall for half of the time on your face and for the rest of the time on the back of your head. Likewise, as the Moon travels round the Earth, the Sun rises and sets over each part of its surface but, because the Moon takes about a month to travel round the Earth, 'day' and 'night' on the Moon each last for about a fortnight.

How Long Is a 'Moonth'?

The Moon takes 27·3 days to travel once round the Earth but takes 29·5 days to pass through its cycle of phases, from New to New, or from Full to Full. Why are these periods different?

If the Earth did not move round the Sun, the lunar month would be exactly equal to the Moon's orbital period and New Moons would occur at intervals of precisely 27·3 days. However, in the time it takes the Moon to go once round the Earth, the Earth itself has moved through an angle of about 27° along its orbit round the Sun. Therefore, after 27·3 days, the Moon has not moved round far enough to be in line with the Sun again. It has to continue round its orbit for a further couple of days before Moon and Sun are again in line and the next New Moon occurs.

The Vexed Problem of the Calendar

Our calendar is rather odd. We have four months of 30 days, seven months of 31 days and one month, February, which has 28 days in three years out of four, but 29 days every fourth year! The dates of religious festivals, such as Easter, seem to roam back and forth through the calendar by up to a few weeks from year to year. Why is it all so complex?

The ancient nomadic hunting peoples had no need of precise ways of recording date or time. The cycle of the Moon's phases provided a convenient natural time unit, easy to observe and short enough to enable people conveniently to remember what was happening one or two cycles or 'months' ago. As civilizations developed, important ceremonies and events were timed to coincide with particular phases of the Moon.

For practical purposes it was necessary to have a whole number of days in a month but, unfortunately, a lunar month (29·53 days) does not contain a whole number of days.

When agriculture began to develop, the annual cycle of seasons became of paramount importance and so an annual calendar, tied to the seasonal changes in the position of the Sun, was required. As the Babylonians and Egyptians realized, some 5000 years ago, the year contains 365 days, but does not consist of a whole number of lunar months. Twelve lunar months of 29·5 days add up to 354 days, 11 days short of a year. The Egyptians adopted a delightfully simple approach, by having a year consisting of twelve 30-day months with five extra days at the end of each year. In the Muslim calendar, the year consists of 12 lunar months and is, therefore, 354 days long. Because the actual year is 11 days longer than this, the start of a given month advances through the year at the rate of 11 days per year and passes through all four seasons in about 33 years.

Careful long-term observations of the star Sirius, the brightest star in the sky, which they called 'Sothis', led the Egyptians to conclude that the year itself did not consist of a whole number of days. The Egyptian agricultural year began in July with the annual flood of the Nile, which irrigated the land. Around 4500 years ago, it was noticed that this event coincided with the time each year when 'Sothis' first became visible in the eastern sky just before sunrise (this event is known as the 'heliacal' rising of Sirius). As the years went by, however, the 365-day 'year' became more and more out of step with the heliacal rising and the seasons. The Egyptians eventually concluded that the year consists of $365\frac{1}{4}$ days so that the civil calendar and the seasons would get progressively out of step at a rate of one day every four years.

Many attempts were made to reconcile the calendars, some sensible, some bizarre. In 45 BC, Julius Caesar tried to bring order to the chaotic Roman calendar by adding an extra day every fourth year to take up the accumulating effect of the extra quarter day that each year contained; this is similar to the 'leap year' system that we use today. He used alternating months of 31 and 30 days' duration apart from February (29 days) but the logic for the latter months was disrupted by the Emperor Augustus who insisted that 'his' month, August, should also contain 31 days and reduced February to 28 (except in leap years).

However, because the year is not precisely $365\frac{1}{4}$ days long, then, even with leap years, the months began slowly to slip through the seasons. By 1582, the discrepancy had become significant, and Pope Gregory XIII decreed that ten days should be deleted from October of that year to bring the calendar back into line with the seasons. He also altered the rule for calculating leap years. Normally a leap year occurs when the year is divisible by 4 without remainder (for example, 1996 will be a leap year, but 1997 will not be). Gregory decreed that century years should be leap years only when the number of the century was itself divisible by 4; thus 1600 was a leap year, but 1700, 1800 and 1900 were not. However, the year 2000 will be a leap year. With this amendment, the Gregorian calendar, as used today, is tied accurately to the seasonal year with an error of only one day in 3000 years.

Although Gregory's reform was quickly adopted in Catholic countries, Protestant nations regarded the proposal with great suspicion. Great Britain did not adopt the reform until 1752, by which time the discrepancy was eleven days and, even then, there were riots when people thought that eleven days were being stolen out of their lives.

Earthshine

Seen from the surface of the Moon, the Earth is a most impressive sight, much more colourful than the Moon is in our skies. Because the Moon keeps the same face turned towards the Earth all the time, the Earth seems to hang almost stationary in the sky. The Earth shows phases, changing from a thin crescent to 'Full' and back to 'New' in the same period of time (29·5 days) as the lunar cycle. When the Moon is 'New', it lies between the Sun and the Earth. Seen from the Moon, the Earth is 'Full' at that instant. Conversely, when the Moon is Full, the Earth appears 'New'.

The Earth appears about four times larger in the lunar sky than the Moon appears in ours. The barren, rocky, dusty Moon reflects only about 7 per cent of incoming sunlight, but because of the presence of clouds, snow and ice the Earth, on average, reflects about 33 per cent. Taking these factors into account, the 'Full Earth' in the lunar sky is about 100 times brighter than the Full Moon in ours. When the Moon is in its crescent phase, which occurs when the Earth is nearly full in the lunar sky, we can see the effects of Earthshine on the Moon. The dark part of the Moon's globe is faintly illuminated by Earthlight, giving the impression of a faintly-luminous disc cradled in the bright sunlit crescent, a phenomenon which is called 'the Old Moon in the New Moon's arms'.

The Old Moon in the New Moon's arms

When the Moon is a thin crescent, the Earth is nearly 'Full' in the lunar sky and sufficient Earthlight – sunlight reflected from the Earth – falls on the lunar surface to enable the whole lunar disc to be seen. Although the earthlit region is very faint, the major lunar features – bright highlands and dark plains – can be identified.

High Moon – Low Moon

In winter, the Full Moon seems very high in the sky, but in summer it remains low down, near to the horizon. Why should this be so?

The Moon is always fairly close to the ecliptic (the apparent path of the Sun in the sky). In summer, the Sun is well north of the celestial equator and, at noon, is high in the sky, reaching its greatest altitude at the summer solstice. The Full Moon is always on the opposite side of the sky from the Sun and so, when the Sun is high in the sky at noon, the Moon must be low in the sky at midnight. Six months later, the positions are reversed. The Sun, at the winter solstice, is well south of the celestial equator and even at noon remains low down over the southern horizon. The Moon, on the opposite side of the sky, will be well north of the celestial equator and high in the sky.

Harvest Moon and Hunter's Moon

In September, when the Sun is near the autumnal equinox (the point where the ecliptic crosses the celestial equator from north to south), the Full Moon, on the opposite side of the sky, will be close to the vernal equinox (where the ecliptic crosses the celestial equator from south to north). The Sun and the Full Moon will both be on or close to the celestial equator and so, when the Sun is setting almost exactly due west, the Moon will at that instant be rising in the east and will remain visible all night long, setting when the Sun next rises.

Relative to the background stars, the Moon moves from west to east, but, because the ecliptic is tilted by 23.5° to the celestial equator, the

Moon will also be moving quite rapidly northwards when it is close to the vernal equinox. The eastwards motion of the Moon causes it to rise about 50 minutes later, on average, each consecutive evening. However, the effect of moving the Moon northwards is to cause it to spend more time above the horizon than below and this tends to make it rise earlier and set later. When Full Moon occurs with the Moon close to the vernal equinox, its northwards motion goes a long way towards compensating for the progressively later rising caused by its west-to-east motion. In these circumstances, for a few days around Full Moon, there is only a small difference in the time of moonrise on consecutive evenings. Six months later, in spring, the delay between successive rising times of the Full Moon will be at its maximum.

The Full Moon that occurs nearest to the date of the autumnal equinox is known as the Harvest Moon because it occurs around harvest time, and because the Moon rises as soon as the Sun sets and, for a few days, rises at almost the same time. In the days when harvesting was done by hand and artificial lights were not available, the favourable Moon gave enough light to enable farm workers to continue to cut the crop and stack the sheaves until long after the Sun had set. Nowadays, of course, combine harvesters and powerful lights enable harvesting to continue throughout the night and the whole process can be done at a rapid pace as soon as the crop is ready and the conditions are right. Nevertheless, the romance of the Harvest Moon remains for all who care to enjoy its gentle light on those last evenings of late summer.

A similar situation, though less marked, occurs a month later and, because traditionally it is the hunting season, this phenomenon is called the Hunter's Moon.

Harvest Moon (right)

The Full Moon is always on the opposite side of the sky from the Sun. In September, around the time of the autumnal equinox, the Sun lies close to the celestial equator and the Full Moon occurs when the Moon, too, is on or close to the celestial equator. The Moon rises more or less due east at the same instant as the Sun sets in the west and remains above the horizon for 12 hours, providing illumination throughout the night. Because this occurs around the traditional harvest time, when it was necessary to work into the night to get the harvest in as quickly as possible in case bad weather should arrive and damage the crop, this phenomenon is called the Harvest Moon.

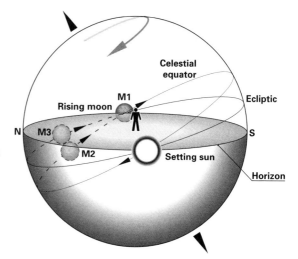

Harvest Moon rising (below)

The Harvest Moon rises more or less due east (M1) at sunset. The Moon's path round the Earth keeps it at all times quite close to the ecliptic. In September the Moon is close to the vernal equinox, the point where the ecliptic passes from south to north of the celestial equator (see above). If the Moon moved, instead, along the celestial equator, by the next evening it would be at position M2 and would rise about 50 minutes later. Because the Moon has actually moved to M3 it has only a short extra distance to travel before again rising above the horizon. For this reason, at that time of year, the Moon rises only a little later each evening for a few consecutive evenings.

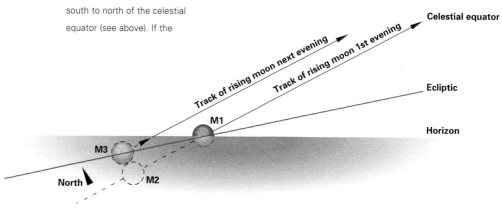

Wandering Nodes and Ancient Lunar Observatories

On midsummer's day, the Sun rises as far to the north of east and sets as far to the north of west as it can, while on midwinter's day it rises and sets as far south of east and as far south of west as it can. The rising and setting points of the Sun repeat these same cyclic changes year after year, but the motion of the rising and setting points of the Moon is much more complex.

The orbit of the Moon is tilted to the plane of the ecliptic by an angle of about 5° and crosses the ecliptic at two points called nodes; the ascending node is where the Moon crosses the ecliptic from south to north and the descending node is where the Moon crosses the ecliptic from north to south. Because of the gravitational pulls of Earth and Sun, the positions of the nodes gradually shift along the ecliptic, making a complete circuit of the sky once every 18·6 years.

This curious cycle affects the rising and setting points of the Moon and the height to which it can rise over the horizon. The combination of the tilt of the Moon's orbit with the tilt of the ecliptic allows the declination of the Moon to reach maximum values of 28·5° north and south of the celestial equator once every 18·6 years (this occurs when the tilt of the ecliptic (23·5°) and the tilt of the lunar orbit (5°) add directly together, which happens when the ascending node of its orbit coincides with the vernal equinox). The Moon will reach its maximum possible altitude above the horizon when its declination is 28·5°N and its minimum possible altitude, two weeks later, when its declination will be 28·5°S. When the Moon is as far north as it can get, it rises as far to the north of east and sets as far to the north of west as it possibly can; when the Moon is as far south as it can get, it rises as far to the south of east and sets as far to the south of west as it can. These positions are known, respectively, as 'the greatest northern moonrise (moonset)' and 'the greatest southern moonrise (moonset)'.

Despite the great complexity of the Moon's motions, some archaeo-astronomers believe that at least some of the ancient megalithic stone circles and alignments were set up to keep track of the rising and setting points of the Moon.

One possible example is Castle Fraser, a stone circle in Aberdeenshire, Scotland. This is a recumbent circle, a circle of standing stones that includes a massive horizontal one (the 'recumbent' stone). When the major southern moonset occurs, seen from Castle Fraser the Full Moon will reach a maximum altitude of only about 4° and will seem to roll along the top of the recumbent stone. We may never know for certain whether this, or other circles such as Temple Wood in Argyllshire, were really used as ancient lunar observatories, but there are certainly good grounds for thinking that they may have been. No doubt other ceremonies and rituals took place at these mysterious places, but why would the ancient astronomer-priests have been keen to keep track of the shifting position of the Moon to the horizon and ecliptic? Perhaps they were trying to work out the 'danger periods' when eclipses were most likely to happen.

Eclipses

An eclipse of the Sun occurs when the Moon passes directly in front of the Sun and wholly or partly blocks out its light. An eclipse of the Moon takes place when the Moon passes into the shadow cast by the Earth. Even today,

Conditions required for eclipses to occur

An eclipse of the Sun occurs when the Moon passes directly between the Sun and the Earth and an eclipse of the Moon occurs when the Moon passes into the Earth's shadow. Because the Moon's orbit is tilted at an angle to the Earth's orbit **a**, the New Moon's cone of shadow usually misses the Earth. Likewise, at Full Moon, the Moon usually passes above or below the Earth's shadow. An eclipse can only happen **b**, if New or Full Moon occurs when the Moon is near one of its nodes (N1 or N2), the points where the Moon crosses the plane of the Earth's orbit. Only then can the Moon's shadow fall on the Earth (solar eclipse) or the Earth's shadow fall on the Moon (lunar eclipse).

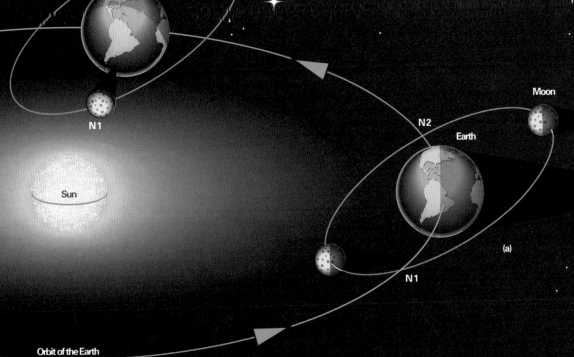

(b)

N2

N1

Sun

N2

Earth

Moon

(a)

N1

Orbit of the Earth

Solar eclipse (below)

The cone of shadow cast by the Moon consists of two parts – the umbra and the penumbra. The umbra is a cone of dark shadow within which the Sun is completely obscured. An observer inside the umbra will see a total eclipse of the Sun. Because the umbra only just reaches as far as the Earth, a total eclipse can be seen only from a tiny part of the Earth's surface. The motion of the Moon along its orbit, combined with the Earth's rotation, causes the Moon's shadow to race across a narrow strip of the Earth's surface – the (total) eclipse track. The much wider penumbra is a region within which only part of the Sun's disc is hidden; an observer within the penumbra will see a partial eclipse.

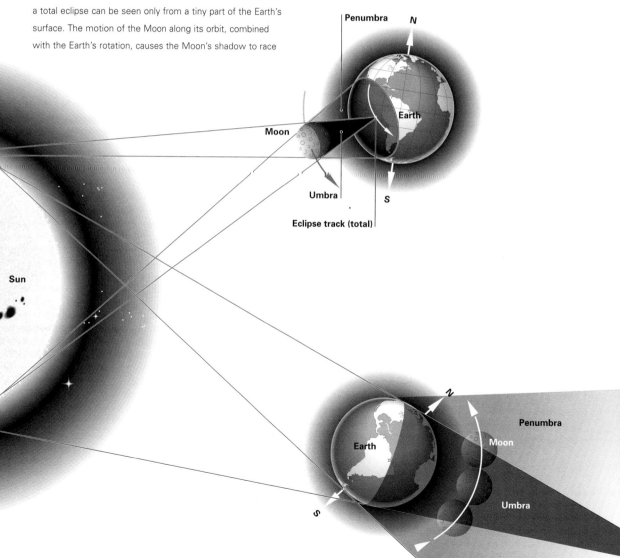

Penumbra N

Earth

Moon

Umbra

S

Eclipse track (total)

Sun

N

Penumbra

Moon

Earth

Umbra

S

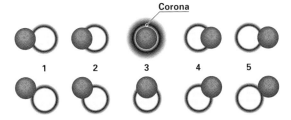

Corona

1 2 3 4 5

Solar eclipse sequence

(above)
At a total solar eclipse (upper sequence) the Moon's disc advances across the face of the Sun from west to east (which is actually right to left as you look southwards towards the sun). The dark 'bite' grows (5), (4) until totality (3) takes place. At this stage, the dazzling face of the Sun is completely covered and the faint corona is seen around the dark lunar disc. After a few minutes, the Moon's disc begins (2), (1) to slide away and the corona vanishes. Even at the centre of a partial eclipse (lower sequence), the Moon covers only part of the solar disc.

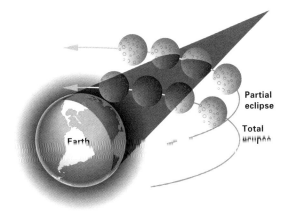

Partial eclipse

Total eclipse

Earth

Lunar eclipse (left)

Because the Earth is about four times larger than the Moon, its shadow is wider, and stretches further, than that of the Moon. If the Moon passes completely into the Earth's umbra, a total eclipse of the Moon will occur. In principle, sunlight should be completely cut off from the Moon and the Moon should disappear. In practice, the Earth's atmosphere bends some sunlight around the edge of our planet, so that faint illumination still falls on the Moon and it does not, normally, vanish completely. A partial eclipse is seen when only part of the Moon enters the umbra. If the Moon only enters the penumbra very little darkening occurs.

Total and partial lunar eclipse (above)

During a total lunar eclipse the Moon moves into the Earth's umbra from west to east. More and more of the lunar disc darkens until, when completely inside the umbra, the whole Moon is dark (or, at least, very faint). During a partial eclipse, the Moon only partly enters the Earth's umbra so that part of its disc remains brightly illuminated at all times.

when we know what causes them and can predict precisely when they will occur, eclipses are among the most dramatic spectacles of nature. To early humankind they must have been terrifying and capricious events. Astronomer-priests who developed or knew of ways of predicting eclipses would have held great power in the eyes of their people.

If the Moon followed an orbit that lay exactly in the same plane as the Earth's orbit, the Moon would pass directly between Earth and Sun at each New Moon and would pass into the Earth's shadow at every Full Moon. An eclipse of the Sun would occur at every New Moon and an eclipse of the Moon at every Full Moon. In fact, because of the tilt of its orbit, the Moon usually passes a little way above or below the Sun at New Moon and a little above or below the Earth's shadow at Full Moon. An eclipse of the Sun or Moon can occur only when Sun, Moon and Earth lie almost exactly on a straight line and this can only happen when the Moon is close to one of the nodes (the points where the lunar orbit crosses the ecliptic).

The shadow cast by the Moon, or by the Earth, consists of two parts, the umbra and the penumbra. The umbra is a cone of dark shadow; for anyone inside this cone, the Sun will be completely hidden and a total eclipse of the Sun will be observed. The penumbra is a wider zone from within which the Sun is only partly hidden; anyone inside the penumbra will see a partial eclipse of the Sun.

By a strange quirk of nature, the Sun and the Moon look almost exactly the same size in the sky. In reality, the diameter of the Sun is nearly 400 times greater than that of the Moon but, because the Sun is also nearly 400 times further away, they look the same apparent size in our skies. Because of this, the cone of dark shadow cast by the Moon (the umbra) only just reaches as far as the Earth. As the Moon passes in front of the Sun,

Total eclipse of the Sun
(opposite)
These images of the total solar eclipse of 16 February, 1980, show the dark disc of the Moon advancing over the face of the Sun until totality (centre) occurs and the corona – the Sun's faint outer atmosphere – appears. Thereafter, the Moon slides off the solar disc. Although the Moon edges from west to east (right to left) relative to the Sun, the Earth's rotation causes each successive solar image to appear further to the west (right).

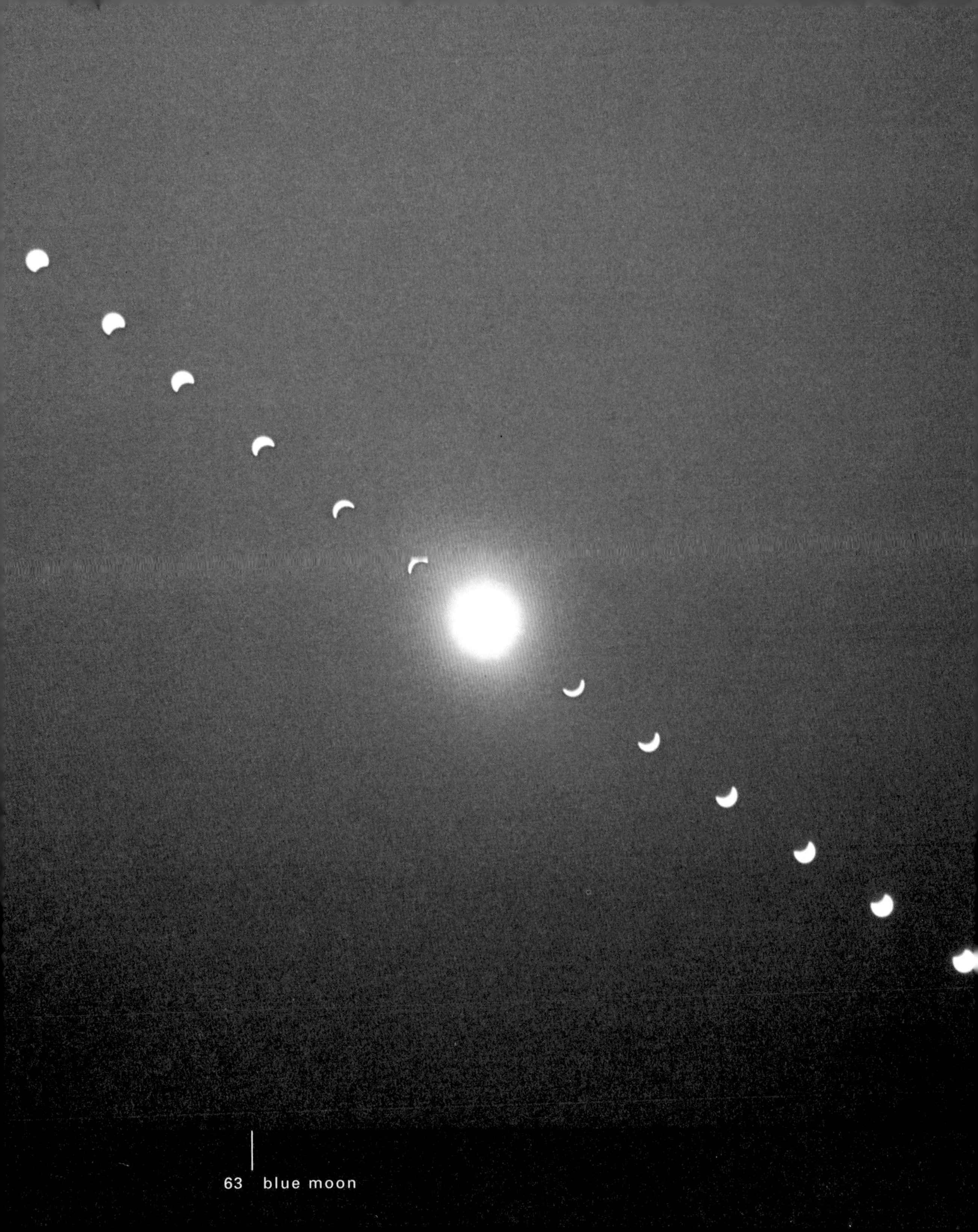

the tip of its umbra races across a narrow strip of the Earth's surface – seldom as much as 250 kilometres (150 miles) wide – and it is only from within this narrow strip that a total eclipse can be seen.

A total eclipse of the Sun begins when the Moon starts to edge in front of the Sun, producing a small dark 'bite' out of the Sun's brilliant disc. The 'bite' gradually grows until, with the onset of totality, the Sun's disc vanishes completely. During totality, the sky goes moderately dark, the brighter stars become visible (demonstrating in the most dramatic fashion that the stars really are still there in daytime) and the glow of the Sun's outer atmosphere – the corona – comes clearly into view around the dark disc of the Moon. Truly, it is a magnificent and awe-inspiring sight, one of the most impressive of all natural phenomena and one which impels dedicated eclipse-watchers time after time to travel all over the globe just to catch a glimpse of this amazing cosmic drama.

Totality can never last for much more than 7 minutes, and often is of much shorter duration than that. Totality ends when the continuing eastwards motion of the Moon exposes the first slim sliver of the solar disc and brilliant sunlight floods back into the sky. Thereafter the dark lunar disc gradually edges off the face of the Sun.

Anyone located outside the cone of dark shadow but within the much wider penumbra will see a partial eclipse, where the Sun is only partly covered by the Moon.

Because it is visible only from a very narrow strip on the Earth's surface, a total solar eclipse is a rather rare event at any particular place; the last one visible in England was in 1927, the next will be in 1999. On the planet as a whole, however, solar eclipses are not infrequent. There can be as many as five in one year and there must be at least two.

Eclipses of the Moon

Because the Earth is about four times larger than the Moon, its shadow is wider and extends further. If the Moon passes completely into the umbra, a total eclipse of the Moon will occur. Although we might expect the Moon to vanish completely, because its supply of sunlight has been cut off by the Earth, in practice the Earth's atmosphere bends rays of sunlight so that a small amount of faint light still reaches the lunar surface.

If only part of the Moon's disc enters the umbra, only part of the lunar disc will be in dark shadow, and a partial eclipse will be seen.

Although eclipses of the Moon are less frequent than eclipses of the Sun, you are more likely to see a lunar eclipse than a solar one because a lunar eclipse can be seen simultaneously from an entire hemisphere of the Earth whereas a solar one – particularly a total eclipse – can be seen only from a limited region of the Earth's surface.

Total eclipse of the Moon
This occurs when the Moon passes into the central part of the Earth's shadow. This sequence shows (right to left) five successive stages in the total lunar eclipse of June 5–6th, 1982. Sunlight bent round the edge of the Earth by our planet's atmosphere casts a dim reddish glow on the Moon even during the 'total' phase of the eclipse.

The Ceaseless Tides

The tides are familiar to anyone who lives by or visits the seaside, and to all those who go to sea for business or pleasure. Over a period of about 6 hours, the sea's edge advances up the beach, demolishing painstakingly-constructed sandcastles as it does so, then, having reached its 'high water' level, it retreats over the next 6 hours or so until it reaches 'low water'. Small sea creatures become trapped in rock pools, and small boats dry out on their moorings. Then, with inevitable certainty, the water begins to advance once more.

On average, there are two high waters and two low waters in a period of 24 hours 50 minutes; if, for example, high water occurred at midday (1200 hours) one day, it would occur 50 minutes later (1250) the next day, and so on. The rise and fall in the depth of water between 'high water' and 'low water' is known as the 'range'.

The tides are caused mainly by the gravitational pull of the Moon on the Earth and its oceans. Its pull on the oceans that face the Moon is greater than its pull on the centre of the Earth itself, and this difference in attraction causes the water on the Moon-facing hemisphere to flow into a bulge underneath the Moon. The Moon attracts the solid body of the Earth more strongly than the water on the far side; the water on the far side tends to get 'left behind' and flows into a bulge on that side.

If the Moon were stationary, a point on the Earth's surface would pass through a bulge at 12-hourly intervals, at the same times every day. However, because the Moon is moving round the Earth, the direction of the bulges follows the Moon and so the Earth has to rotate through more than a full circle before a particular point will return again to the Moon-

Tidal bulges and the Earth's rotation

The Moon's gravity raises two tidal bulges in the oceans **a**, one facing the Moon and the other on the Earth's far side. The Earth's rotation carries a particular place through the two bulges giving two 'high waters' (1, 3) and two 'low waters' (2, 4) per day. However, because the Moon moves round the Earth and the tidal bulge follows the Moon **b**, the Earth has to turn through more than 360° before a place returns to the first high-water bulge (5). High water, therefore, occurs about 50 minutes later each successive day.

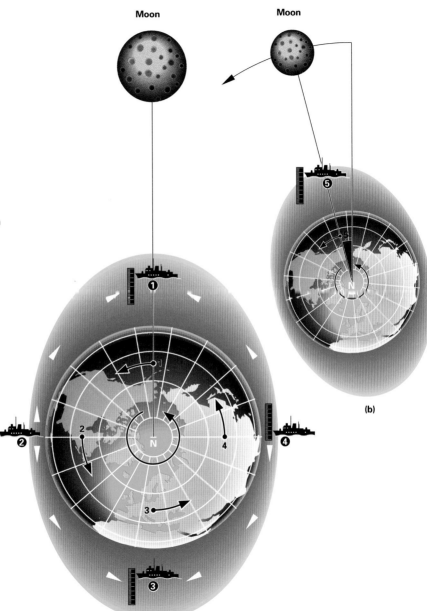

Moon

Moon

(a)

(b)

facing bulge. The extra rotation takes about 50 minutes, so the tides occur, on average, 50 minutes later each day.

In the oceans, far from land, the heights of the bulges are small, only about 60 centimetres (2 feet), but closer to land, in shallower more confined waters and especially in estuaries and bays, local conditions greatly affect the rise and fall and the speed of the tidal flow. Typically, the difference in depth between high water and low water is a few metres.

The Sun also affects the tides but, because it is much further away, its 'tide-raising force' is only about two-fifths of that exerted by the Moon. When Sun and Moon are closely lined up, as at New Moon and Full Moon, their tidal forces add together causing bigger bulges and larger tides, which are known as spring tides; at spring tides, high water is higher and low water is lower than normal. When Sun and Moon are pulling at right angles, as at first and last quarter, their effects partially cancel each other out, causing a smaller bulge and producing neap tides which have a much smaller range.

The Moon as a World

About one quarter of the Earth's diameter and with a mass of only $\frac{1}{81}$ of that of the Earth (81 moons would be required to balance the Earth on a set of cosmic scales), the Moon itself is a bleak and barren world.

The main surface features are craters, mountains and dark, dusty lava plains. The major dark plains are easily visible with the naked eye and make up the shape of the 'man in the moon'. The dark plains were called 'seas' by the early telescopic astronomers of the seventeenth century because they thought that these areas actually were seas and oceans. In reality, there is not a single drop of liquid water on the Moon's arid surface but, despite this, the Latin names of the so-called 'seas' (for example, *Mare Imbrium* or Sea of Rains) have been retained on present-day maps.

The bright 'highland' regions are peppered with huge craters, some of which are up to about 250 kilometres (150 miles) in diameter. They are thought to have been excavated by the impacts of asteroids and meteorites – huge lumps of rocks and metal that struck the lunar surface with explosive violence when the Moon was young. A few craters, such as Tycho, Aristarchus and Copernicus, are surrounded by 'rays', bright, light-coloured material that sprayed out over the lunar surface when these, more recent, craters were formed. The bright splash of rays around Copernicus is easily seen with the naked eye near Full Moon.

The Moon has had a turbulent past but is now an inert world where little, if anything, changes, apart from the occasional impact of a meteorite or man-made space probe.

Observing the Moon

With the naked eye alone, there is much to do. Try keeping track of the changing phase by making a sketch and noting the time on every available night; keep a lookout, too, for the faint glow of Earthlight on its 'dark' surface. Discover for yourself how much later the Moon rises on each consecutive evening and see how the angle between Sun and Moon grows as the phases progress; note too how the position of the Moon shifts against the background stars.

By reference to distant objects such as trees, houses or hills, or by taking compass bearings, note how the position of moonrise or moonset shifts north and south in a periodic way. You will soon begin to see the patterns of behaviour which so intrigued the ancient sky-watchers and builders of stone circles. Watch, too, how the altitude of the Moon increases and decreases with the seasons. Look out for the closely similar rising times of the Harvest Moon and for the large daily changes in moonrise time at other seasons of the year; for example, the delay in successive risings of the Full Moon is greatest in March.

With binoculars or a small telescope, there is a wealth of detail to be seen. The boundary between day and night on the lunar surface is called the 'terminator'. Between New Moon and Full Moon, it represents the line on the Moon's surface where the Sun is rising, whereas between Full and New it is the line along which the Sun is setting. Mountains, valleys and craters are best seen when they are close to the terminator because they then cast long shadows that cast them into sharp relief. At Full Moon, craters and valleys are hard to make out, because the Sun is shining down vertically onto the Moon and shadows are least.

The Moon is one of the easiest astronomical subjects to photograph and much can be done with the simplest of equipment and ordinary medium-speed film (100 or 200 ISO rating is fine). Slide film gives better results, but print film, if more convenient, will do fine. Set up your camera on a tripod, focus for 'infinity', point it at the Moon and click off a few exposures of around $\frac{1}{1000}$th to $\frac{1}{64}$th of a second (depending on the phase). Try a range of exposures – some may be over-exposed and others under-exposed, but at least one ought to be about right. If you haven't tried this before, you will be amazed by the smallness of the Moon's image on the photo. A telephoto lens will show a larger, more detailed, image but will require longer exposure and the motion of the Moon may cause blurring.

The planets Mercury and
Venus accompany the
Moon in this evening sky.
Mercury is the lowest
star-like object while
Venus shines brilliantly in
the upper left.

chapter

the moving planets

The stars that hang like jewels in the blackness of the sky seem eternal and unchanging. Year after year, the same star patterns, or constellations, come round into the night sky at the same seasons and, even over timespans of centuries, show no perceptible alterations to the naked eye. Yet, since the dawn of recorded history, sky-watchers have been puzzled and perplexed by five bright starlike points that behaved very differently – they moved around relative to the background of fixed stars and so came to be known as 'wandering stars', or planets (the word 'planet' derives from the Greek word *planetes*, meaning 'wanderer').

Although they rise in the east and set in the west, just like the stars, the planets slowly move, night by night and month by month, through the constellations of the zodiac. When best-placed, three of them – Mars, Jupiter and Saturn – remain visible all night long. The other two 'wanderers', Mercury and Venus, behave rather differently. They remain relatively close to the Sun and may be seen either in the early morning sky before sunrise or in the evening sky after sunset, but never at midnight.

Mercury is not easy to see from temperate latitudes because, when visible to the naked eye, it is always low down in the morning or evening twilight. Venus, however, is unmistakable. Far brighter than any other star or planet, it is the most brilliant object in the sky apart from the Sun and the Moon and has often been mistaken for a UFO. When well-placed, it can remain visible for several hours, in the eastern sky before dawn or in the western sky after sunset. When visible in the evening sky it is often known as the 'Evening Star' and when it appears in the morning sky as the 'Morning Star'. The strange comings and goings of this dazzling object so puzzled some of the ancient astronomers that they wondered if Venus might be two different objects.

The motions of Mars, Jupiter and Saturn are equally peculiar. For most of the time, they slowly edge their way from west to east relative to the background stars but, from time to time, each slows down, stops, runs 'backwards' for a while, then forwards again. Humankind struggled for thousands of years to explain these bizarre wanderings of the planets.

The Nature of the Planets

Nowadays we know that the planets are bodies which, like the Earth, travel round the Sun, each in its separate orbit. There are nine planets altogether. They are, in order of distance from the Sun: Mercury, Venus, the Earth, Mars, Jupiter, Saturn, Uranus, Neptune and Pluto. The last three are too faint to be seen with the naked eye and were not discovered until long after the invention of the telescope – Uranus in 1781, Neptune in 1846 and Pluto in 1930. The system of bodies comprising the Sun, the nine planets, the moons of those planets, and everything else that revolves round the Sun, is called the solar system.

Like the Moon, the planets shine by reflecting sunlight; unlike stars, they have no light of their own. The stars are so far away that they look like tiny points of light, even when viewed through the most powerful telescopes, but the planets, which are much nearer to us, can readily be seen as discs in quite modest telescopes.

The time taken for a planet to travel once round the Sun is its orbital, or 'sidereal' period. A planet closer to the Sun moves at a higher speed, and has less distance to travel, than one which lies further away. Consequently, the more distant the planet, the longer its orbital period; their periods range from 88 days (Mercury) to nearly 248 years (Pluto).

Mercury and Venus – the Inferior Planets

Mercury and Venus are known as the inferior planets because they are closer to the Sun than we are and therefore are always inside the Earth's orbit. If you imagine their orbits as rings around the Sun, it is easy to see that these planets will always appear fairly close to the Sun in the sky, rising before the Sun when they are on its west side and setting after the Sun when they are on its east side.

When a transit can occur

A transit occurs when an inferior planet (Mercury or Venus) passes directly between the Sun and the Earth. On such occasions, the planet will be seen as a small black dot crossing the face of the Sun. Each inferior planet's orbit is slightly tilted so that when Sun, planet and Earth come into line the planet usually passes either below (A) or above (C) the Sun.

The two points at which a planet's orbit crosses the plane of the Earth's orbit are known as nodes, N1 being the ascending node, where the planet passes from south to north and N2 the descending node, where the planet crosses from north to south. A transit can occur (B, D) only if the planet passes between Sun and Earth when it is at or close to one of its nodes.

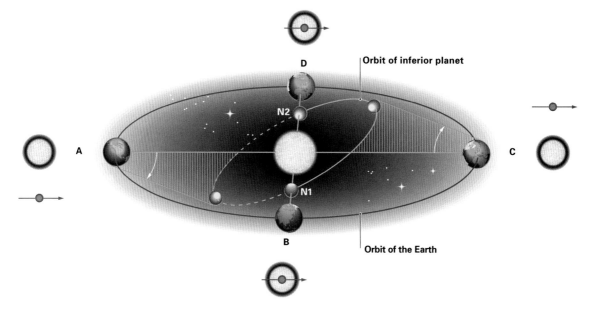

Orbit of inferior planet

Orbit of the Earth

Each inferior planet periodically overtakes the Earth, passing between the Sun and the Earth as it does so. The close alignment of two (or more) bodies in the sky is called a conjunction; when Mercury or Venus passes between the Sun and the Earth, it is said to be at inferior conjunction. Because their orbits are slightly tilted to the plane of the Earth's orbit (Mercury by 7° and Venus by about 3°), Mercury and Venus usually pass a little way above or below the Sun when they reach inferior conjunction. Occasionally the alignment will be such that Mercury or Venus will pass exactly between Sun and Earth and may then be seen as a tiny black disc crossing the face of the Sun. Such an event is called a transit.

The two points at which a planetary orbit crosses the plane of the Earth's orbit are known as nodes, and a transit can occur only if inferior conjunction happens when a planet is at or very close to one of the nodes. Transits of Mercury are not particularly rare. The last one occurred in November 1993 and the next one will take place on 15 November 1999. Transits of Venus are much rarer. The last one was in 1882 and the next will not take place until 2004.

After inferior conjunction a planet moves to the west of the Sun and becomes visible in the morning sky before sunrise. The angle between the Sun and the planet (the 'elongation') increases to a maximum (28° for Mercury and 47° for Venus) and then begins to decrease again as the planet continues around its orbit towards the far side of the Sun. Eventually the planet passes behind the Sun and is then said to be at superior conjunction. Thereafter, it re-emerges on the eastern side of the Sun and follows the Sun across the sky, setting after the Sun. It is then visible in the evening sky after sunset, setting progressively later than the Sun as it moves out towards greatest elongation. Thereafter, the angle between the planet and the Sun decreases again until, once more, it passes between Sun and Earth at the next inferior conjunction.

Both Mercury and Venus pass through a cycle of phases as they move round the Sun. Like the Moon, half of a planet's globe is lit up by the Sun and the other half is in shadow. When a planet is at inferior conjunction – between Sun and Earth – the Earth-facing hemisphere is dark, just like the Moon at new Moon. As the angle between Sun and planet increases, we start to see part of the illuminated hemisphere, beginning as a thin crescent which grows to a 'half-moon' appearance by the time the planet has reached greatest elongation west. Thereafter, as the planet progresses towards the far side of the Sun, we see a larger and larger proportion of the sunlit side until, when the planet reaches superior conjunction, we see a fully-illuminated disc just like 'Full Moon'. At that point the planet is too close to the Sun to be seen. When the planet emerges on the east side of the Sun, the illuminated phase begins to decrease, eventually shrinking to a thin crescent as the planet approaches inferior conjunction and vanishing when the planet passes between Sun and Earth.

Small telescopes or even binoculars will show the phases of Venus.

Beyond the Earth – the Superior Planets

Mars, Jupiter, Saturn, Uranus, Neptune and Pluto are known as the superior planets because they lie further from the Sun than we do and are always outside the Earth's orbit. They cannot pass between the Sun and the Earth and so can never be seen in transit.

Because they are more distant, and move more slowly than the Earth, our planet overtakes each superior planet at regular intervals. On such occasions, Sun, Earth and planet come into line, with the planet on the opposite side of the Earth from the Sun. The planet is then said to be at opposition. Because it is opposite the Sun in the sky, and the Sun is at upper transit (due south and at its highest point above the horizon) at noon, the planet will be at upper transit at midnight. At such times, the planet is visible all night long.

After overtaking the planet, the Earth pulls ahead of it and the angle between the planet and the Sun begins to decrease until, eventually, the Earth is on the far side of the Sun from the planet and, seen from the Earth, the planet is at superior conjunction. Throughout this time, the planet sets progressively earlier until it vanishes into the evening twilight and passes behind the Sun. The planet then reappears on the west side of the Sun and begins to rise before the Sun, becoming visible in the dawn twilight. As the Earth gradually begins to catch up with the planet, the angle between the Sun and the planet increases, and the planet rises progressively earlier. Eventually, by the time the next opposition comes round, it rises around sunset and sets around sunrise.

Loops in the Sky

Because all the planets travel round the Sun in the same direction, the normal motion of a planet, relative to the background stars, is from west to east; this is known as direct motion. However, if you plot the changing positions of Mars on a star map, over a year or so, you will notice something decidedly strange. First of all, its apparent speed will vary but, more peculiarly, as it approaches opposition, Mars will stop, run 'backwards', or retrograde, from east to west for some time, then stop again and resume its

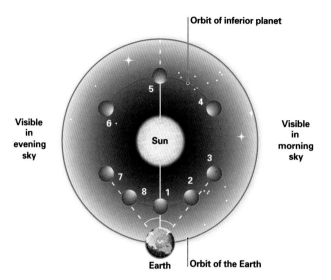

Orbit of inferior planet

Visible in evening sky

5
4
6
Sun
3
7
2
8 1

Visible in morning sky

Earth | **Orbit of the Earth**

Elongation and phases – inferior planet

When an inferior planet passes between the Sun and the Earth (1) it is said to be at inferior conjunction. At this point the Earth-facing side is dark. The planet moves to the west of the Sun and shows a phase that grows from a thin crescent to a 'half-moon' appearance when the angle between Sun and planet is maximum (greatest elongation west: 3) and 'full' when the planet reaches the far side of the Sun (superior conjunction: 5). Thereafter, the planet moves to greatest elongation east (7) and returns to inferior conjunction (1).

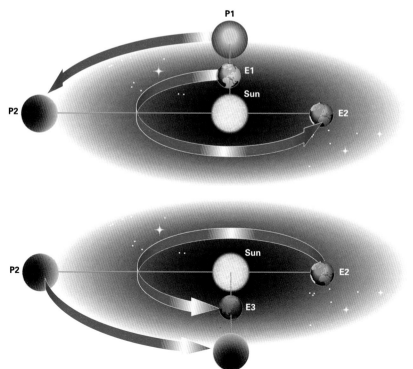

P1
E1
Sun
E2
P2

Sun
P2
E2
E3
P3

Opposition and conjunction – superior planet

A superior planet is at opposition when Sun, Earth (E1) and planet (P1) are in line with the planet on the opposite side of the Earth from the Sun. The Earth then moves ahead of the slower-moving planet until eventually the Earth (E2) is on the opposite side of the Sun to the planet (P2); the planet is then said to be at superior conjunction. The next opposition occurs when the Earth (E3) catches up again with the planet (P3).

onward progress from west to east. The planet seems to trace out a flattened loop in the sky before moving on. It will trace out another 'loop' at the next opposition and as it continues to move, will trace out loops from time to time. This motion was a complete mystery to the early astronomers.

Changing View of the Planets

To the ancient sky-watchers, it seemed self-evident that the Earth was at the centre of the universe and that everything else – Sun, Moon, planets and stars – revolved round the Earth. The ancient Greek civilization, which flourished round the eastern Mediterranean between about 700BC and AD 200, made many advances in humankind's understanding of the universe but, apart from a few independent thinkers, remained firmly wedded to the geocentric (Earth-centred) view.

The Greeks developed the notion that the Sun, Moon and planets move round the Earth on circular paths. The circle was considered to be a perfect geometrical form, and each planet was believed to move along its circle at a constant, unchanging, speed. A key problem with this idea was that the planets did not move at a constant rate in the sky and, moreover, they traced out these inexplicable loops from time to time.

Clearly, the simple idea that the planets moved at constant speeds along Earth-centred circles was not good enough and further development of the theory was essential. Around 260 BC, Apollonius proposed that a planet might move round an epicycle, a small circle, the centre of which moved round the Earth on a larger circle called the deferent. The general motion of the planet relative to the stars was caused by the motion around the deferent while the periodic planetary loops were caused by the motion of the planet round the epicycle. Hipparchus, the outstanding observational astronomer of the second century BC, developed the concept of the eccentric – a circle whose centre was offset to one side of the Earth. Even if the planet moved at a constant speed along its circle, it would seem to move at a varying speed because its distance from Earth would vary.

All these ideas, and more, were brought together in the second century AD by Claudius Ptolemaeus, better known as Ptolemy, in a marvellous book which came to be known as the Almagest, which means 'the greatest'. Ptolemy used combinations of epicycles and eccentrics, together with an invention of his own (the equant) to try to describe the motions of the planets. Although his system was complicated and far from perfect, it was remarkably successful at predicting planetary positions.

Revolution

Despite its many imperfections, the Earth-centred view was almost universally accepted until the scientific revolution of the sixteenth and seventeeth centuries finally pushed it aside.

The first step was taken by a Polish cleric, Nicolaus Copernicus (1473-1543), who proposed that the Sun was at the centre of the universe and that the Earth and all the other planets travelled round it in circular paths. By taking this step, he could immediately explain why the planets traced out their retrograde loops in the sky. It was simply a matter of relative motion. Each time the Earth overtakes a planet, the planet seems for a while to run backwards relative to distant objects (the stars) just as a slow-moving vehicle seems to run backwards, relative to you, when you are overtaking it. But, because he persisted in believing in perfect circular motion, he was still unable precisely to explain the observed motions of the planets in the sky.

Because his heliocentric (Sun-centred) theory flatly contradicted the geocentric view that had long been held by the established churches, Copernicus held back from publishing his theory until 1543, the year of his death. His book, *De revolutionibus orbium coelestium* ('On the revolutions of the heavenly spheres'), laid the foundations for what has come to be known as the Copernican Revolution.

Gradually, the Copernican theory began to gain support. One of its key supporters was Galileo Galilei (1564-1642), the great Italian astronomer and natural philosopher who, among his many accomplishments, was the first to use the recently-invented telescope to great effect and who laid some of the key foundations of the science of mechanics. With his telescopes he saw craters and mountains on the Moon, spots on the Sun, discovered four moons moving round Jupiter, observed the phases of Venus and showed that the Milky Way is made up of countless numbers of stars. His observations of Jupiter's moons showed that the Earth was not the only centre of motion in the universe, and the phases of Venus demonstrated that Venus must travel round the Sun.

Galileo became an outspoken exponent of the Copernican theory – too outspoken for his own good as it transpired. In his book, *Dialogo sopra i due massimi sistemi del mondo, Tolemaico e Copernico* ('Dialogue…concerning two world systems, Ptolemaic and Copernican'), he discussed arguments for and against the Copernican theory by means of a discussion between two characters, Salviati representing the Copernican (and Galileo's) view, and Simplicio, representing

The Ptolemaic Earth-centred universe

According to Ptolemy (circa AD 140), the Earth lay at the centre of the universe and the Moon, Sun and planets all revolved round the Earth. Beyond the planets lay the sphere of stars. Each planet moved round a small circle (the epicycle), the centre of which revolved round the Earth. The full Ptolemaic system was more complex than is shown here.

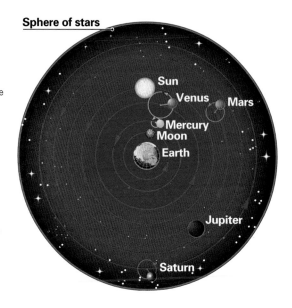

Sphere of stars

Sun
Venus
Mars
Mercury
Moon
Earth
Jupiter
Saturn

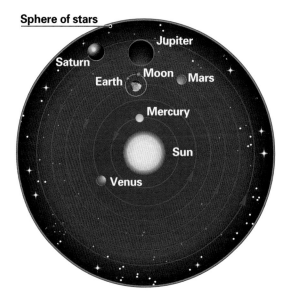

Sphere of stars

Jupiter
Saturn
Earth
Moon
Mars
Mercury
Sun
Venus

The Copernican sun-centred (heliocentric) universe

According to Copernicus (1473–1543), the Sun was at the centre of the universe and all the planets, including the Earth, travelled round the Sun in circular orbits. The Moon travelled round the Earth and the sphere of stars lay beyond the planets. The Copernican system still required devices such as epicycles and has been simplified here for clarity.

the traditional Earth-centred view. The Dialogue, and Galileo's strongly-expressed opinions, put him in such bad odour with the leaders of the Catholic church and, in particular, with Pope Urban VIII who was persuaded that Simplicio was a caricature of himself, that in 1633 he was put on trial before the Inquisition and forced publicly to recant the 'heresies' that he had been proclaiming. From then on, until his death in 1642, he was effectively confined to a state of 'house arrest' in his villa at Arcetri, in the hills overlooking Florence.

Others were not convinced by this new heliocentric view. One of these was Tycho Brahe (1546-1601), a Danish nobleman and an outstanding observational astronomer of his time. Although he had no telescopes, he was able to construct instruments that enabled him to measure the positions of stars and planets with unprecedented accuracy. He could not accept the idea of a moving Earth but could see the advantages of having the planets move round the Sun, and so devised a compromise theory of his own (the Tychonic theory) which had the Sun moving round the Earth and the planets moving round the Sun.

Although his theory did not stand the test of time, Tycho's accurate observations of the planets provided the data that eventually enabled the German astronomer Johannes Kepler (1571-1630) to solve once and for all the riddle of planetary motion. In 1600, Tycho invited Kepler to join him in Prague to work on the motion of the planet Mars. Over the next eight years, Kepler tried all kinds of combinations of circles, epicycles, deferents, eccentrics and equants, to try to fit its observed motions.

Although by these means he was able to get agreement between observation and theory to an accuracy of about 8 minutes of arc (about an eighth of a degree), this was not good enough for Kepler.

Finally, after some seventy attempts, he found the answer. The orbit of Mars had to be an ellipse, an oval curve rather than a circle, with the Sun at one focus of the ellipse (a point off to one side of the centre) rather than at its true centre. His results relating to Mars were published in 1609 in his book, *Astronomia Nova* ('The New Astronomy'), and were later extended to include the other planets. He developed three laws of planetary motion, now known as 'Kepler's laws', which in essence stated the following:

First law: Each planet travels round the Sun in an elliptical orbit with the Sun at one focus of the ellipse.

Second law: The speed of a planet varies as it moves along its orbit, faster when closer in and slower when further away.

Third law: The square of a planet's orbital period is directly proportional to the cube of its mean distance from the Sun. For example, a planet 4 times as far from the Sun as we are would have a period, in years, equal to the square root of 4 cubed. Now 4 cubed = $4 \times 4 \times 4 = 64$ and the square root of 64 is 8; therefore its orbital period would be 8 years. Kepler's third law was particularly important because it established the relative distances of the planets from the Sun. It would then only be necessary to find the actual distance of one of them in order to find the distances of them all.

Although Kepler's ideas were not immediately accepted by all supporters of the Copernican theory (Galileo, for one, seems never to have accepted the idea of elliptical motion), his system's simplicity and its success in describing and predicting the movements of the planets ensured that it soon became widely adopted by the scientific community.

Kepler finally ended thousands of years of belief in the central position of the Earth and the circular motion of the planets. Astronomy, physics and human philosophy could never be the same again.

Why Do the Planets Move as They Do?

Kepler had established how the planets move. It fell to the English scientist, Isaac Newton (1642-1727), to explain precisely why the Moon and planets move in the ways that they do.

Newton's investigations into the idea of gravity began in 1665 when he had returned to his home at Woolsthorpe, near Grantham, because Cambridge University had been closed on account of the Great Plague. He realised that a constant force acting towards the centre was necessary to keep a body moving in a circle. The story goes – and it may even be true! – that he was prompted by watching an apple fall from a tree to consider whether the force that caused the apple to fall might be the same force that kept the Moon in its orbit round the Earth.

Newton went on to show that the force of attraction ('gravitation') between any two bodies depends on the product of their masses divided by the square of the distance between them. If the distance is doubled, the force is reduced to a quarter of its previous value.

He then proved that a body acted on by the gravitational pull of a massive body will follow an elliptical path in accordance with Kepler's laws. This law applies equally to the motion of the Moon round the Earth, the motions of the planets round the Sun and the motions of stars in distant parts of the universe. Newton's law of gravitation is a universal law – it applies to all bodies everywhere in the universe.

Newton published this law, and much more besides, in 1687 in his book *Philosophiae naturalis principia mathematica* ('The Mathematical Principles of Natural Philosophy'), which was, without question, one of the greatest scientific works of all time.

How Big Is the Solar System?

The earliest known estimate of the size and distance of the Sun was made by the Greek philosopher Anaxagoras (500–428 BC). He assumed the Earth to be flat and deduced from his observations that the Sun was a 'red hot stone' larger than the Peloponnese, the peninsula on which the Greek city of Athens stands, and at a distance of, in today's terms, about 6500 kilometres (about 4000 miles).

A much better estimate was made two centuries later by another Greek astronomer, Aristarchos. He deduced that the Sun was about 20 times more distant than the Moon and showed, therefore, that the Sun is larger than the Earth. More than a century later, again, Hipparchus deduced from observations of the size of the Earth's shadow on the Moon that the Moon lay at a distance of 30 Earth-diameters, a remarkably accurate result. From this, he concluded that the distance to the Sun was, in today's terms, about 7,700,000 kilometres (4,800,000 miles).

Ptolemy, in the second century AD, increased the estimated distance but Copernicus used a smaller value. Kepler, in 1618, gave a figure of 22,500,000 kilometres (14 million miles) but, as it turned out, this was still far too small. What was needed was an accurate method of establishing the mean distance between the Sun and the Earth, a distance which is called the astronomical unit. An accurate knowledge of the astronomical unit was vitally important because our entire knowledge of the scale of the universe rested, as it still does, on the precision with which this figure can be determined.

The keys to solving the problem were the principle of parallax and Kepler's laws of planetary motion.

Parallax

The principle of parallax is well-known to surveyors and, indeed, was known in ancient Greek times. Try this experiment now: Hold up one finger at arm's length and, with your left eye closed, line up your finger on a distant object – say a tree or a chimney. Now, without moving your finger or your head, close your right eye and open your left. Your finger will no longer be lined up with the distant object. The reason for this is very simple: your eyes are separated by a few centimetres and so each eye is looking at a foreground object, like your finger, from a different position along a slightly different direction.

If you measure the angular change in position of your finger and you measure the separation between your eyes, you can use simple trigonometry (or a scale drawing) to calculate the length of your arm (admittedly, you could just measure your arm with a measuring tape, but the principle is valid!).

The same principle can be applied to measuring the distances of the planets. If the same planet is observed from two widely-separated locations, it should be possible to measure a slight change in its position relative to the background stars. Knowing the separation between the observing sites, the distance of the planet can be found.

From a knowledge of the orbital periods of the planets, we can apply Kepler's laws to find their relative distances from the Sun in terms of the Earth's distance; for example, a planet with an orbital period of 8 years must be at a distance of 4 astronomical units, four times the Earth's distance. From Kepler's laws we can find the distance of each planet from the Sun in astronomical units and can work out their distances from the

A transit of Venus

This took place in 1874 and was the first to be recorded photographically. Venus is the black disc towards the upper left-hand side of solar disc, close to the cross-wires.

Earth, also in astronomical units. If we can then measure the actual distance between the Earth and just one planet, we will automatically be able to work out the others.

Venus proved to be the key planet in the application of this process.

The Astronomical Unit

Edmond Halley, discoverer of the famous comet and contemporary of Isaac Newton, proposed in 1716 that the best way to measure the astronomical unit would be by means of a transit of Venus. He argued that observers at different places on the Earth's surface would see the black disc of Venus follow different tracks across the face of the Sun, and by measuring the angles between these tracks, the parallax of Venus, and hence the distance of both Venus and the Sun, could be measured.

When the next transit was due, in 1761, no less than sixty-two scientific expeditions were despatched to different parts of the globe to view this phenomenon. Even greater scientific effort was concentrated on the 1769 transit. Among the more charismatic expeditions on this occasion was the voyage commanded by the English

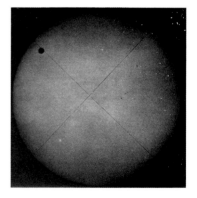

explorer, Captain James Cook, who after obtaining good observations of the transit from the island of Tahiti, continued his voyage, charting the coasts of New Zealand and the eastern seaboard of Australia, and claiming both of these lands as British possessions.

The data acquired by the various expeditions that observed the 1761 and 1769 transits was finally analysed by the German astronomer Johann Encke, who calculated a value of 153 million kilometres (95 million miles) for the astronomical unit, a value that differs by just 2 per cent from today's accepted figure.

Parallax, transits and the astronomical unit

The principle of parallax **a**, is straightforward. Two widely-separated observers (A and B) on the Earth's surface look at a nearby planet along slightly different directions and see that planet at slightly different positions (PA and PB) against the background stars. If the angular shift in position is measured and the distance D is known, the distance of the planet may be calculated. At a transit of Venus **b**, observers A and B will see the dark disc of Venus cross the face of the Sun along different track. Determination of the angular separation between them enables the distance of Venus, and hence the distance of the Sun, to be found.

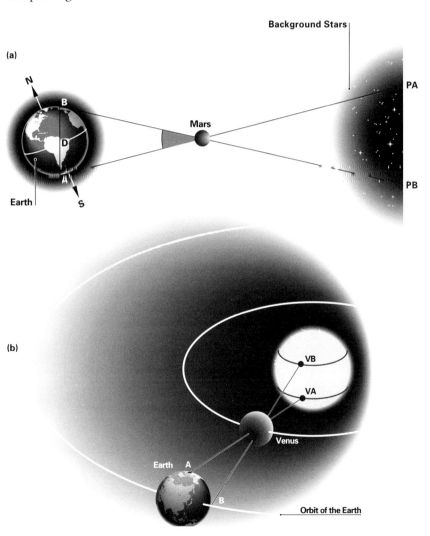

The value was further refined at the next transits, in 1874 and 1882. In the early part of the twentieth century, observations of asteroids were used. These are small rocky bodies that follow independent orbits round the Sun. Because some of them pass closer to us than any of the planets, their parallaxes can be measured with greater accuracy than those of the planets.

Since the 1960s, astronomers have been able to measure planetary distances with great precision by means of radar. The principle is very simple. A pulse of microwave radiation, travelling at the speed of light (300,000 kilometres (186,000 miles) per second) is beamed from the Earth to the target planet. It bounces back and returns, much weaker, to the Earth. By measuring the time taken to complete the round trip, multiplying by the speed, and dividing by two (in going out and back the signal has covered twice the distance to the planet), we can find the distance. By using this technique, astronomers have discovered that the value of the astronomical unit is 149,597,893 kilometres (92,955,600 miles). We now know the distance of the Sun to within 1 kilometre – a far cry indeed from the days of Anaxagoras, Ptolemy, or even Kepler.

The Solar System to scale

Distances in the Solar System are vast, but it is not too difficult to visualize the relative distances and sizes of the planets if we think of a scale model. For example, if the Sun were to be represented by a ball 14 centimetres ($5\frac{1}{2}$ inches) across, the Earth would be a pinhead, 1.2 millimetres ($\frac{1}{20}$ inch) across, at a distance of 15 metres (50 feet) from 'the Sun', Saturn would be a 1.1-centimetre marble at a range of 143 metres (470 feet) and remote Pluto would be tiny pinpoint some 600 metres (2000 feet) away.

the moving planets

The Planets as Worlds

Centuries of telescopic observations and decades of close-range investigations by spacecraft have given us detailed knowledge of each planet.

Mercury is a barren, cratered, airless world, only two-fifths of the Earth's size. Being so close to the Sun, it gets extremely hot. At noon, near the planet's equator, the temperature climbs to more than 450°C, whereas at night it plummets to 180° below zero.

Venus is similar to the Earth in size but has a dense, cloud-laden atmosphere composed mainly of the heavy gas carbon dioxide. Carbon dioxide is a 'greenhouse' gas – very effective at trapping heat that otherwise would escape from a planet's surface back into space. For this reason, the temperature at the surface of Venus is maintained at over 450°C. The clouds are composed of droplets of sulphuric acid and the pressure exerted at the planet's surface by the great weight of its atmosphere is 90 times that here on Earth. Despite its beautiful appearance and association with the goddess of Love, Venus is a thoroughly hostile place!

The Earth itself is unique among planets in having large quantities of liquid water on its surface, free oxygen in its atmosphere, and in supporting a huge variety of life-forms.

Mars, the red planet, is only about half the Earth's size and has a very tenuous atmosphere. It has craters, valleys and huge extinct volcanoes on its dusty surface. Although no liquid water flows on its surface, there is some water locked up in the polar ice caps, and there are features on its surface which look remarkably like dried-up river beds. Although at one time many people thought that Mars might be inhabited we now know that there is no sign of life of any kind on this neighbour world.

Jupiter is the largest and most massive planet of all, and is completely different in nature from the Earth. Its huge globe is large enough to contain well over 1000 Earths, and, beneath its deep cloud-laden atmosphere, the body of the planet is composed mainly of liquid hydrogen and helium. Giant Jupiter has at least sixteen moons, four of which, the Galilean satellites, can be seen with small telescopes or binoculars.

Saturn is similar to, but slightly smaller than, Jupiter. Its most distinctive feature is the immense system of rings that surround it. Composed of billions of individual particles, ranging in size from blocks of rock and ice larger than houses down to particles smaller than grains of sand, the rings lie above the planet's equator and have a diameter equivalent to two-thirds of the distance between the Earth and the Moon.

Uranus and Neptune are both considerably smaller than Jupiter but are still about four times the size of the Earth. Like Jupiter and Saturn, they have deep cloud-laden atmospheres and contain a great deal of hydrogen. These frigid worlds of the outer solar system also contain a lot of ice of various kinds. Pluto is a tiny icy planet considerably smaller than the Moon. It follows a markedly elliptical orbit which carries it from far beyond to just inside Neptune's distance. It made its last close approach to the Sun in 1989 and until 1999 will remain closer in than Neptune.

Observing the Planets

With the exception of Mercury, which can usually only be seen low down for a few days around each greatest elongation, the naked-eye planets are bright and easy to identify. Venus is unmistakably brilliant, and both Mars and Jupiter appear brighter than any star when well-placed. Saturn is a bright object, with a yellowish hue. If you get to know the constellations, you will soon recognize when a planetary 'interloper' is present, but in any case astronomy magazines and many newspapers give monthly guides to where the planets are to be found in the sky.

Having found them, watch how their positions change from week to week and month to month and see for yourself the perplexing motions which so greatly puzzled the early generations of sky-watchers.

Binoculars, if you can hold them steady enough, will easily reveal the changing phases of Venus and the shifting positions of the four brightest moons of Jupiter.

With a reasonably-sized telescope all kinds of phenomena will be revealed. Jupiter and Saturn are particularly rewarding to study. Jupiter's disc is readily visible in the smallest of telescopes, and modest instruments will show several of the major cloud belts which encircle this giant world. The only long-lasting feature in Jupiter's atmosphere is the Great Red Spot, a reddish oval cloud feature, itself larger than the Earth. The changing positions of the major satellites can easily be followed and, from time to time, one or more of the satellites will pass behind or in front of the planet's disc or disappear into its shadow.

Saturn's rings are an amazing sight, even through a small telescope, and few people fail to be impressed the first time they swim into view. Two or three rings can be seen with quite modest telescopes, together with Saturn's giant moon Titan and some of the smaller ones.

Mars is rather small, and harder to observe, but at a close opposition, dark markings and the polar ice caps can be seen. Occasionally, the surface features will be partly or wholly obscured by dust storms in the Martian atmosphere.

Note:

If you are keen to get involved there is no limit to the amount of observational work you can do with the planets, but, whatever your level of interest, it is well worth spending a little time outside to identify our neighbouring worlds and watch their silent motions against the much more distant stars.

chapter

to boldly go...

This illustration from Peter Apian's *Geographica*, published in 1533, shows cross-staffs being used to measure distant buildings and the separations between stars.

The early mariners navigated with the aid of a compass, which gave the direction in which they were heading, and by making the best estimates that they could of the distance they had travelled. When European navigators set forth to explore the oceans, following the pioneering lead of the Portuguese prince, Henry 'the Navigator', in the fifteenth century, they began to develop astronomical methods of determining their position at sea. But how do we define the position of a particular place?

Latitude and Longitude

The position of a place on the Earth's surface is described by latitude and longitude. Latitude describes position in a north-south direction and longitude in an east-west direction. A globe of the Earth, or a map in an atlas, is covered by a grid of lines that mark out latitude and longitude.

The latitude of a place is the angle between the equator, the centre of the Earth, and the place. The latitude of the equator itself is 0°, and the latitudes of the north and south poles are 90° north (N) and 90° south (S), respectively. The latitude of London is about 52°N, that of St Louis, Missouri, is about 39°N, while that of Melbourne, Australia, is about 38°S. Points of equal latitude lie on circles ('lines of latitude') parallel to the Earth's equator and circles of latitude become progressively smaller as we move from the equator towards either of the poles.

The other part of the grid is provided by lines, called meridians, that join the north and south poles and cross the equator at right angles. The longitude of a place is the angle, measured east or west, between the Greenwich meridian (the meridian that passes through the old Royal Observatory at Greenwich, England) and the meridian that passes through

Latitude and longitude
The latitude of a place (A) on the surface of the Earth is the angle (BCA) between the equator and the place. The longitude of place (A) is the angle between the Greenwich meridian [the circle that passes through both poles and Greenwich (G)] and the meridian passing through (A).

the place. The longitude of Greenwich is precisely 0° and every other place that lies along this meridian is also at longitude zero.

Longitude is measured in degrees (and fractions of a degree) from 0° to 180° eastwards (E) and from 0° to 180° westwards (W) from the Greenwich meridian. Moscow, for example, is at longitude 38°E, and Melbourne at 145°E, whereas New York is at 74°W and St Louis 90°W. Longitude 180°E coincides with longitude 180°W on the opposite side of the Earth from the Greenwich meridian.

Finding your Latitude

Finding your latitude is relatively simple. An approximate method is to locate the Pole Star, Polaris, and measure its altitude   the angle between the horizon and the star. The altitude of the north celestial pole is always equal to your latitude; for example, if you are at the north pole of the Earth (latitude 90°N), the pole is vertically overhead (its altitude, therefore, is 90°), whereas if you are at the equator (latitude 0°), the celestial pole is right down on your horizon (altitude 0°). Polaris does not coincide exactly with the true pole, but does lie within 1° of it. A measurement of the altitude of Polaris will give you your latitude to within a degree or so; this corresponds to an error of about 60 nautical miles (approximately 100 kilometres) on the Earth's surface. The fifteenth-century Portuguese navigators used this approach in their early ocean voyages.

Another approach is to measure the altitude of the Sun at noon.

During the morning, the Sun rises higher in the sky, reaching its maximum altitude at noon; it then sinks back towards the horizon in the afternoon. The noon altitude of the Sun on any particular day depends on the latitude of the place; further south than the UK, the noon Sun is higher in the sky, whereas further north, it is lower.

If we know what the noon altitude of the Sun will be at, say, Greenwich and we find that it is, for example, 5° higher at our location, we can immediately tell that we are 5° south of Greenwich; if the noon altitude is less than the Greenwich value, we must be north of Greenwich. In practice, because the Sun is further north in the sky in summer than in winter, the noon altitude of the Sun depends not only on the observer's latitude but also on the season of the year. In order to use the noon altitude of the Sun to determine our latitude, we need to know the declination of the Sun (its angle north or south of the celestial equator) on each day of the year. This information is well-known to astronomers, and is contained in tables that navigators carry with them.

The altitude of the Sun is measured by means of the sextant, a device that uses mirrors attached to a pivoting arm to move the image of the Sun, seen by the observer, until it coincides with the horizon; the amount of movement is measured on a graduated scale and this gives the altitude of the Sun directly. The sextant is a complex precision instrument.

The early navigators, however, used a much simpler device called a cross-staff which, in essence, consisted of two pieces of wood in the form of a cross. The observer looked along from one end of the longer arm of the cross and slid the shorter arm to and fro until one end coincided with the horizon and the other with the Sun. The angle could then be read off on a scale marked out along the long arm. The smaller the angle, the further the short arm had to be slid along the long arm.

A series of observations was made around the middle of the day, starting before and continuing until after noon. Because the altitude of the

Sun increases before noon and decreases thereafter, the observations would reveal the noon altitude. From this, and a knowledge of the Sun's declination, the latitude could be calculated. By these simple means, the early ocean explorers (such as Francis Drake when he sailed the *Golden Hind* from London to America) were able to measure their latitude to within about 30 miles (48 kilometres) or so. In good visibility, land (unless it was low-lying) could be seen by a lookout up the mast, from that sort of range, so, if the aim was simply to make landfall somewhere along the coast of a large land mass, this degree of accuracy was not too bad.

Running Down the Latitude

Finding longitude was an altogether more difficult task and, until the eighteenth century, there was no direct, practicable, way in which a navigator could measure it. Instead, the normal method was to steer well to one side (east or west) of the intended destination then head south or north along a meridian until the correct latitude was reached. This technique was called 'running down the latitude'. The vessel would then turn east or west and sail at a constant latitude until the intended destination hove into view. If heading for a large land mass or continent, the vessel was unlikely to miss it, even if the exact point of landfall was rather uncertain. However, if the intended destination were a smallish island, it would be relatively easy to miss it altogether and errors in navigation could be, quite literally, matters of life or death.

A typical case is the sad tale of Commodore Anson who, in 1741, was ordered to take HMS *Centurion* round Cape Horn to the island of Juan Fernandez, with strict instructions to keep out of sight of the mainland to avoid discovery by the Spanish. When he had run down to about the correct latitude, he guessed that he was east of the island and turned his vessel to the west. When the island did not appear, he turned round and headed back to the east. When he sighted the mainland, he quickly turned round again and resumed his search. But supplies were running low and scurvy broke out among his crew. By the time he finally reached Juan Fernandez, between seventy and eighty of the crew had died. Ironically, on a previous voyage – to Lisbon – this same vessel had been used to test out the prototype of a new device which eventually would solve the problem of longitude determination. But at the time of Anson's voyage, this device was not on board.

The key to the problem lay in the accurate measurement of time.

Longitude and Time

Local noon occurs at the same instant everywhere along the same meridian, but occurs at different times for places east or west of that meridian. For example, when it is noon at Greenwich, the Sun has only just risen in the mid-western United States, and has already set in Indonesia, central China and Mongolia.

The difference between local time and Greenwich time (the time measured by someone on the Greenwich meridian) is determined by the longitude of the place and the rotation of the Earth. Because the Earth rotates from west to east, the Sun will rise earlier, and noon will come earlier, in places to the east of Greenwich, and later at places west of Greenwich. In 24 hours the Earth spins through an angle of 360°; in 1 hour it turns through 15°, and in 1 minute through 15 minutes (′) of angle.

Greenwich meridian

The Greenwich meridian, which marks longitude zero and separates the eastern and western hemispheres, runs through the old Royal Observatory at Greenwich, England, and is marked by a brass strip laid in the ground outside. The meridian passes through a telescope, seen here, called the Airy transit circle. Instruments of this kind were used to time the precise instants at which known stars crossed the meridian. The results were used to regulate clocks.

One hour after crossing the Greenwich **meridian,** the Sun will cross the meridian at longitude 15°W, and 6 hours after Greenwich noon, it will be local noon at longitude 90°W – in places such as St Louis or New Orleans. Conversely, the Sun crosses the meridian 15°E of Greenwich 1 hour before Greenwich noon, and crosses the meridian at longitude 90°E 6 hours before crossing the Greenwich meridian. When it is noon at Dacca, in Bangladesh, it is 0600 (6 a.m.) everywhere along the Greenwich meridian.

At longitude 179°E, local time is virtually 12 hours ahead of Greenwich time whereas at 179°W, local time is almost exactly 12 hours behind Greenwich time. If it is 1200 hours (noon) at Greenwich, it will be 2356 (4 minutes to midnight) at longitude 179°E and 0004 hours (4 minutes past the previous midnight) at longitude 179°W; there is a difference of 23 hours 52 minutes between the local times at 179°E and 179°W. What happens at longitude 180°? There will be a difference of 24 hours between the times registered on clocks that lie immediately on opposite sides of the line. If it is 0000 hours on, say, 15 October, on one side of the line, it will be 0000 hours on 14 October (24 hours earlier) on the other side of the line. For this reason longitude 180° is known as the International Date Line.

The Earth, today, is divided into 24 time zones, each 15° of longitude wide. Clocks advance by 1 hour each time you cross into a new time zone heading east, and go back 1 hour each time you cross a new zone heading west. However, in practice, the time zones take account of national and state boundaries.

Longitude and time

Local time differs from Greenwich time by an amount that depends on the longitude of the place. Places to the east of Greenwich (G) are ahead of Greenwich time and places to the west are behind. Looking down on the north pole of the Earth, **(i)** the Sun is crossing the meridian, and it is therefore noon, at longitude 90° east when it is just rising at Greenwich (longitude 0°). Six hours later **(ii)**, it is noon at Greenwich, sunset at **A** and sunrise at **B** which is 90° west of Greenwich. After a further six hours **(iii)**, it is noon at **B**, sunset at Greenwich and midnight at **A**.

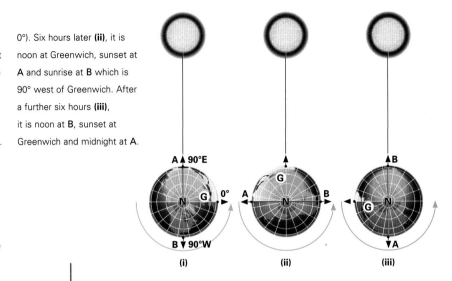

(i)   **(ii)**   **(iii)**

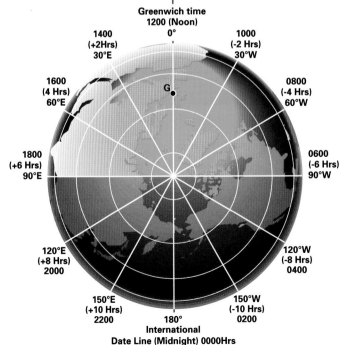

**Greenwich time
1200 (Noon)
0°**

1400
(+2Hrs)
30°E

1000
(-2 Hrs)
30°W

1600
(4 Hrs)
60°E

G

0800
(-4 Hrs)
60°W

1800
(+6 Hrs)
90°E

0600
(-6 Hrs)
90°W

120°E
(+8 Hrs)
2000

120°W
(-8 Hrs)
0400

150°E
(+10 Hrs)
2200

150°W
(-10 Hrs)
0200

180°
**International
Date Line (Midnight) 0000Hrs**

Time Zones

Local times at various longitudes are shown, advancing ahead of Greenwich time with increasing easterly longitude (anticlockwise from the Greenwich meridian) and falling further behind with increasing westerly longitude (clockwise from the Greenwich meridian). When it is 1200 hours at Greenwich it is 0000 hours at longitude 180°. This point is the International Date Line and the date changes by one day as you cross it.

Greenwich Time and Local Time Within the UK

Differences in local time show up over smaller distances too. Lowestoft, on the east coast of England, is at longitude 1°44′E, and Ardnamurchan Point, the western extremity of mainland Scotland, is at longitude 6°14′W. Between these most easterly and most westerly points of mainland Great Britain, there is a difference of nearly 8° of longitude. For this reason, local noon at Ardnamurchan will occur 32 minutes later than at Lowestoft.

Before 1880, clocks normally operated on local time, and local clocks would be 4 minutes behind Greenwich clocks for every degree of longitude west of Greenwich. Since a degree of longitude at the latitude of Greenwich corresponds to an east-west distance about 68 kilometres (42 miles), if you could have have flown westwards at a speed of 68 kilometres (42 miles) every 4 minutes (17 kilometres (10 ½ miles) per minute), or 1000 kilometres (620 miles) per hour from the east coast to the west coast, you would have been able to hear each and every church clock chime the same hour as you passed overhead.

When the horse-drawn Royal Mail coaches started running regular schedules, just before 1800, they ran to a very tight timetable in order that connections could be made with a network of interconnecting coaches. The London to Bristol coach run took about 16 hours and its timetable laid down precise arrival and departure times at each stop on the way. Now, for the first time, the fact that each town operated on its own local time became important. The coachman's watch, set in London, would differ from local time by an increasing amount the further west he went and, by the time he had covered the 190 kilometres (120 miles) to Bristol, would be reading 11 minutes ahead of local time.

The solution adopted by the Royal Mail company was to adjust the coachman's watch so that it ran slow at a rate of 15 minutes in 24 hours on the westward journey (about 10 minutes over a 16-hour trip) and gained 15 minutes in 24 hours during the eastward journey. That way, the coachman's watch would read the correct local time at all points along the route.

The Adoption of Greenwich Time

Although by the middle of the nineteenth century the great majority of public clocks in Great Britain were operated on Greenwich time, legal confusion persisted until 1880 when, by Act of Parliament, Greenwich time was designated the standard time in Great Britain for all official and legal business. Following the international conference, the Greenwich meridian was adopted internationally as the Prime Meridian (longitude zero) for international position-measurement in 1884 and gradually, thereafter, Greenwich Mean Time became adopted as the international standard for time measurement, too.

Time, Longitude and Navigation

The difference between local time and Greenwich time depends precisely on longitude. If local time is ahead of Greenwich time by 4 minutes, the longitude is 1°E, if it is ahead by 1 hour, the longitude is 15°E; if local time is 4 minutes behind Greenwich time, the longitude is 1°W, if it is behind by 1 hour, the longitude is 15°W, and so on. This difference provides the basis of determining longitude at sea.

Railway time

The Great Western railway began running trains from London to Bristol in 1841, and all its stations were linked by the electric telegraph, which allowed instantaneous communication between them. Because of this, the company decreed that all its stations would operate on London (Greenwich) time so that, for example, the 8 a.m. from Bristol to London would leave at 0800 London time, when the local clocks in Bristol would be reading 0749.

To avoid confusion a large clock was set up in a prominent position with two minute-hands – one reading local time and the other London time. The clock is still there today, on Bristol's Corn Exchange Building.

A series of observations of the changing altitude of the Sun would in principle enable the navigator to determine the instant of local noon, and if the navigator also had a clock that kept the exact local time of the port of departure then, by comparing the time of local noon with the time on this clock, the navigator could work out how far east or west of his or her starting point he or she had travelled. If the clock kept Greenwich time, the longitude east or west of Greenwich would be found.

The idea that an accurate portable clock, or chronometer, could be used to find the longitude was first suggested in 1530 by Gemma Frisius. But, in order to know longitude to half a degree, which corresponds to a possible error of 30 nautical miles (50 kilometres) at the equator, the clock would have to be accurate to within 2 minutes (the Earth rotates through half a degree in 2 minutes). Over a 6-week voyage, therefore, the clock could not be permitted to gain or lose more than 3 seconds a day. At that time, clocks were not precise enough to do the job and, since most clocks depended on the swing of a pendulum, they would be useless on the heaving deck of a ship at sea. Watches driven by springs had been invented, but at that time were not remotely up to the job.

Lunar Distances

An alternative approach to determining longitude was to make use of the fairly rapid motion of the Moon in its orbit round the Earth to provide a kind of natural clock. The suggestion, made initially by Johann Werner in 1514 and later promoted by Peter Apian, was that if the positions of the zodiacal stars and the motion of the Moon were accurately known, then the separation between the Moon, the Sun, and known stars in the sky

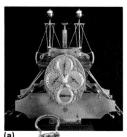

(a)

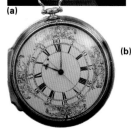

(b)

could be worked out in advance for different dates and times according to local time at the navigator's home port. By observing the angles between the Moon and those stars, or between the Moon and the Sun, when the ship was at sea, the navigator would be able to find out the time at his home port at the instant when other observations would give him the local time. The difference in time would give the longitude difference between the ship and its home port.

The main problems with the method, apart from its sheer complexity, were that the positions of the stars and the motion of the Moon were not known with nearly enough accuracy and the instruments used to measure the angles between the Moon and the Sun or stars – cross-staffs and the like – were not nearly precise enough.

In order to obtain accurate measurements of Sun, Moon and stars, King Louis XIV established the Paris Observatory in 1667 and Charles II paid for the building, in 1675, of the Royal Observatory in Greenwich, England. But, even after forty years, little progress had been made towards the practical attainment of longitude at sea. Consequently, in 1714, the British government established a 'Board of Longitude' that offered a reward of £20,000 to anyone would could devise and demonstrate a method of obtaining longitude at sea to an accuracy of half a degree (about 30 nautical miles or 50 kilometres). Over the ensuing years, the Board received many ideas, some sensible, others impractical and far-fetched, until, finally John Harrison, a self-taught English clock-maker, solved the problem by constructing his marine chronometer, a timepiece that kept sufficiently good time at sea to enable longitude to be determined with real confidence and precision.

chapter

6

starry, starry
night

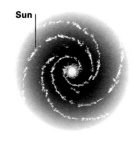

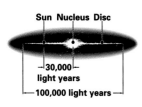

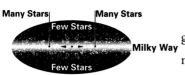

The Galaxy and the Milky Way

Our Galaxy (top) is a spiral system of stars and gas clouds. Seen edge-on (centre) the Galaxy comprises a central bulge surrounded by a flattened disc. The concentration of stars in the disc (below) produces the band of starlight that we call the Milky Way.

Viewed from a really dark site, with clear air and no artificial light, the stars seem to hang like glittering diamonds in the sky. They seem much more brilliant, and they seem somehow to be so much nearer to us. The star-spangled heavens look like a dome suspended over the earth and it is little wonder that that is precisely what many of the ancient peoples thought it really was.

When the Moon is not around, you may also see the Milky Way, a faint diffuse band of light stretching across the sky from horizon to horizon. Binoculars and small telescopes will show that the Milky Way is made up of the combined light of countless individual stars, a discovery that was made in the winter of 1609–1610 when the Italian astronomer Galileo first turned his newly-constructed telescope towards the starlit sky.

It is hard to imagine that each of these distant points of light is a huge globe of incandescent gas, just like our own Sun. Some stars are larger and much more brilliant than the Sun, others are smaller and dimmer, some are hotter, some are cooler. So far as we can tell, the Sun is a very ordinary, middle-aged, middle-of-the-road star. There is nothing exceptional or unusual about it except that it is so much nearer to us than any other star and, of course, we on planet Earth travel round it.

The Sun is one of the 100 billion stars that make up our Galaxy, a huge island of stars spread out in a flattened disc. The Sun is located about three-fifths of the way from its centre to its rim. When we look along the plane of the Galaxy's disc we see vast numbers of distant stars apparently bunched together to give us the Milky Way effect but when we look in other directions we see relatively few stars.

Very large telescopes can detect tens of billions of galaxies each containing billions of stars. The universe truly is a vast place.

Star Patterns

Thousands of years ago, the early sky-watchers began to identify patterns of stars; different cultures had their own myths and legends associated with the stars, and named the brighter stars and star patterns accordingly. In his great book, Almagest, the second-century Greek astronomer, Ptolemy, listed 48 star-patterns, or constellations, all of which are retained on present-day star maps. Since that time, further constellations have been added, including those of the southern skies that were invisible and unknown to the ancient Greeks, so that nowadays the entire celestial sphere is divided up into a grand total of 88 constellations. Some of these are striking and easy to identify, but many are rather obscure.

Many of the constellation names come from ancient Greek mythology. For example, in Greek legend, Andromeda, the daughter of King Cepheus and Queen Cassiopeia, was saved by the hero Perseus from being devoured by a sea monster. Perseus, who had previously slain the Gorgon, Medusa, the sight of whom could turn men to stone, turned the monster to stone by showing it Medusa's head and was then able to rescue Andromeda from the rock to which she had been chained. Andromeda, Cepheus, Cassiopeia and Perseus are all represented by constellations, and Medusa's head is marked by the star Algol within the constellation of Perseus. Some of the more recent constellations have more prosaic names, such as Telescopium (the telescope), or Horologium (the clock).

Many of the individual naked-eye stars were named by Arab astronomers, and the Arabic names, such as Algol, Betelgeuse and Aldebaran, are still in use today. In 1603, the astronomer Bayer devised a system of naming the bright stars in each constellation by letters of the

Greek alphabet, the brightest star in a constellation usually being labelled α (alpha), the second-brightest β (beta) and so on. According to this system, Sirius, the brightest star in the sky, is known as α Canis Majoris ('Alpha' in Canis Major, the Big Dog), Betelgeuse is α Orionis ('Alpha' in Orion) and Algol is β Persei ('Beta' in Perseus).

Identifying Constellations

Although at first the sky may appear to contain a confused jumble of stars, finding your way around becomes relatively straightforward once you have identified a few key constellations and learned how to use these as signposts to many of the others.

Best-known of the northern-hemisphere constellations is Ursa Major (the Great Bear), the seven brightest stars of which make up a distinctive shape rather like a saucepan with a bent handle that is called the Plough or the Big Dipper. The Plough is a convenient signpost to the northern constellations (see Key Map 1). Alpha and Beta are known as 'the pointers' because a line from β through α leads to Polaris, the Pole Star, a fairly isolated star that lies within 1° of the true north celestial pole. Polaris lies about 30° away from the Pointers (it is useful to bear in mind that the spread of your hand at arm's length corresponds to an angle of about 20°) at the end of the tail of Ursa Minor (the Little Bear). If you continue along this line you will come to Cepheus.

The middle star of the 'handle' of the Plough is ζ (Zeta), better known by its proper name of Mizar. A line from Mizar, through Polaris, and extended for a further 30° leads to the 'W-shaped' constellation of Cassiopeia, while extending the curve of the handle for about 30° leads to

Arcturus, the brightest star in Boötes (the Herdsman). Other guide-lines from the Plough are shown below.

Finding stars from the Plough

The Plough, or Big Dipper, is a signpost from which to find other constellations. A line from β ('Merak') through α ('Dubhe') leads to Polaris, the Pole Star, in the constellation of Ursa Minor (the Little Bear). Other lines lead to other constellations.

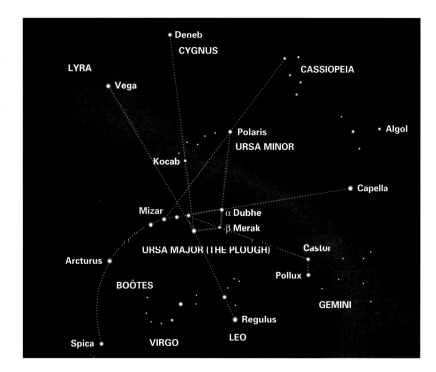

Another valuable signpost to the sky is Orion (the Hunter), the most striking constellation in the heavens and probably the easiest to identify. For those of us who live in the northern hemisphere, Orion dominates the southern part of the night sky throughout the winter months . The basic shape of the constellation is picked out by seven bright stars. At the northeast corner is the bright reddish star, Betelgeuse, while the south-western corner is marked by Rigel, an even brighter bluish-white star. Although Rigel is the brighter of the two, it is labelled β while Betelgeuse is α.

Bellatrix (ν) occupies the north-west corner and Saiph (κ), the south-east. A line of three conspicuous stars, Alnitak (ζ), Alnilam(ε) and Mintaka (δ), marks Orion's Belt.

Follow the line of Orion's Belt down to the south-east and you will come to Sirius, the brightest star in the sky. Follow the line for about 20° to the north-west and you will find Aldebaran (α Tauri), the brightest star in the constellation of Taurus (the Bull). Continue a little further in this direction and you will come to a compact cluster of faint stars called the Pleiades (the Seven Sisters). Most people, under good conditions, can see six or seven stars in this group, but keen-eyed observers can see ten or more. Seen through binoculars, the Pleiades are a splendid sight. Other lines from Orion (see below) lead to Auriga (the Charioteer), Gemini (the Twins) and then on to Leo (the Lion). Having identified Auriga and Taurus you will then be able to find Perseus, and so on.

Finding Stars from the Orion

The striking constellation of Orion is itself easy to identify and provides an excellent guide to finding neighbouring constellations, the Pleiades star cluster and Sirius, the brightest star in the sky. Several guidelines are shown.

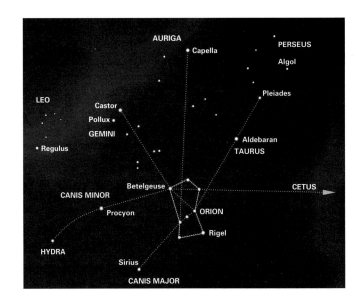

Finding Stars from the Summer Triangle

The 'Summer Triangle' is a pattern of three brilliant stars – Vega, Deneb and Altair – which can be used to identify various other constellations. In the northern hemisphere, it is best seen during late summer and autumn. Vega is the brightest star in the compact constellation of Lyra and the fifth-brightest star in the sky. Deneb is the brightest star in Cygnus and Altair is the brightest star in Aquila. Various sighting lines lead northwards towards Cepheus and Cassiopeia, westward to Hercules, southwards to Sagittarius and eastwards to Pegasus.

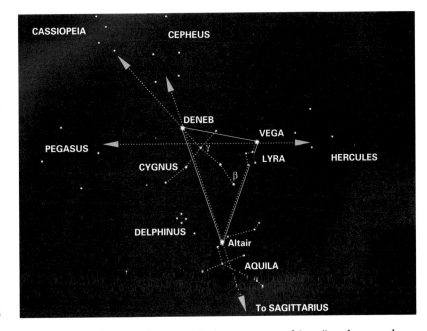

A conspicuous feature of the summer skies (in the northern hemisphere) is a pattern of three brilliant stars known as the Summer Triangle. The Summer Triangle is not a constellation in its own right, but is made up of the brightest stars from three separate constellations, Vega in Lyra (the Lyre), Deneb in Cygnus (the Swan) and Altair in Aquila (the Eagle). Cygnus has a conspicuous cross–shape, and is known unofficially as the Northern Cross. Andromeda lies to the east of the 'Triangle' and Hercules to the west. The Milky Way passes through the Summer Triangle, southwards into Sagittarius (the Archer) and northwards towards Cassiopeia.

When you have identified the Plough, Orion and the Summer Triangle, you will be well on your way to locating most of the other constellations on the sky.

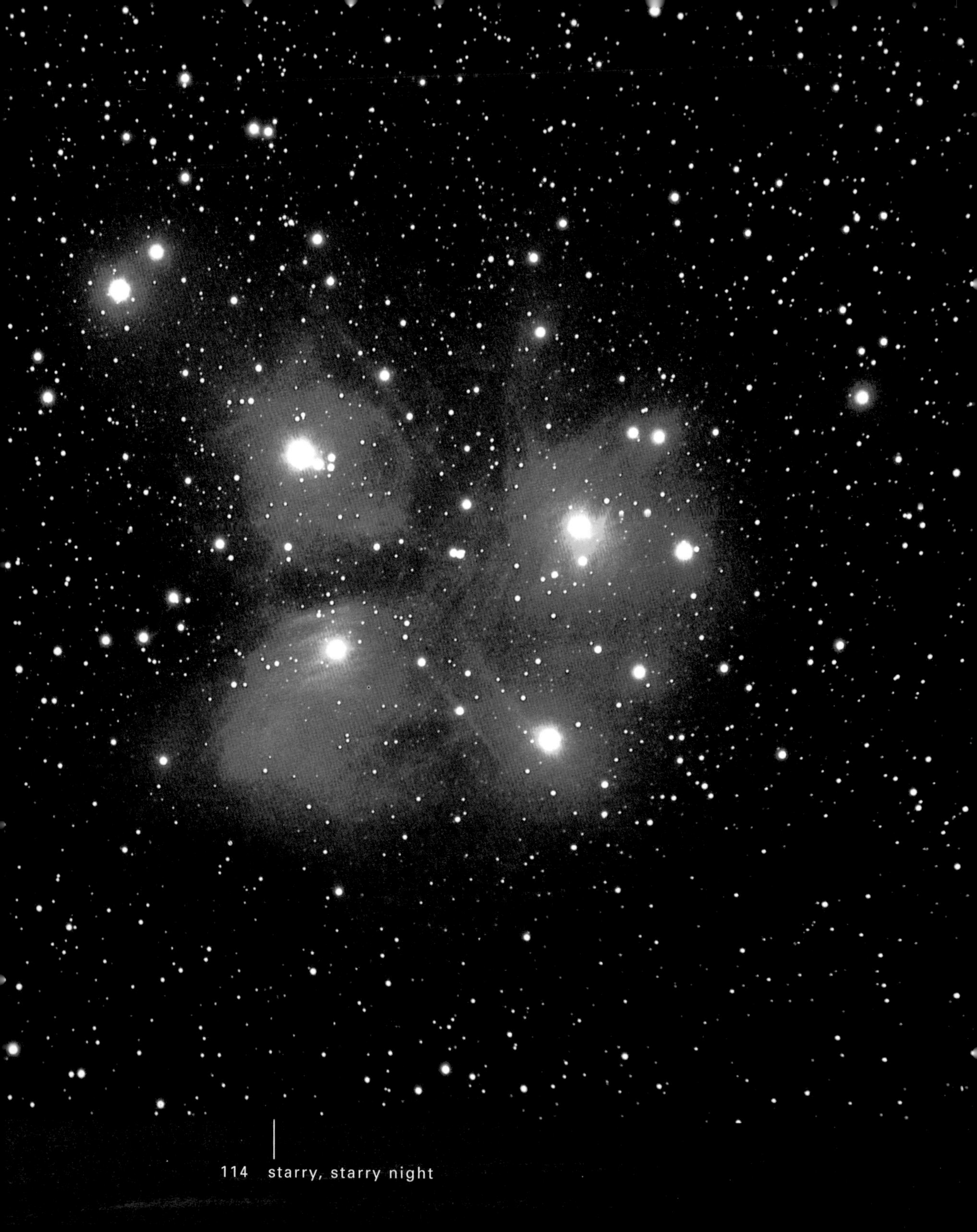

Positions on the Sky

Positions on the sky are described by coordinates rather like latitude and longitude on the Earth.

The angle north or south of the celestial equator (the equator of the sky) is called declination and takes any value between $0°$-$90°$(for a star on the celestial equator) and $+90°$ (for a star at the north celestial pole) or $-90°$ (for a star at the south celestial pole). Betelgeuse is at declination $+7°$ ($7°$ north) and Rigel has a declination of $-8°$ ($8°$ south).

The east-west location is described by an angle called right ascension, which is similar to longitude on the Earth. The equivalent of the Greenwich meridian on the celestial sphere is the meridian that passes through the north and south celestial poles and the vernal equinox. Right ascension is measured eastwards from this meridian.

The Pleiades (left)
The Pleiades star cluster is situated in the constellation of Taurus, some 400 light years from the Earth. As stars go, the Pleiades cluster is young – only about 50 million years old. The cluster is embedded within the remnants of the cloud of gas and dust from which its stars were born. The fuzzy blue patches ('reflection nebulae') around the brighter stars are caused by light reflected from dust particles.

Circumpolar Stars

As the Earth rotates, the celestial sphere appears to rotate from east to west and stars move across the sky, parallel to the celestial equator, tracing out circles around the celestial pole.

If you were standing at the north pole, the north celestial pole would be vertically overhead and stars would trace out circles parallel to the horizon. Stars would neither rise nor set. You would be able to see half of the celestial sphere all of the time, but stars in the other hemisphere would never rise above your horizon. If, instead, you were at the equator, the celestial equator would pass directly overhead, and the two celestial poles would be on the horizon – one due north and the other due south.

Circumpolar stars: the view from below (right)

The view looking north (for an observer in the northern hemisphere). Stars appear to move in circles around the celestial pole. Stars A, B and C, which are sufficiently close to the pole, are circumpolar but star D, which is further away, is not. The altitude of the celestial pole is equal to your latitude and so any star whose angular distance from the pole is smaller than your angle of latitude will be circumpolar for you.

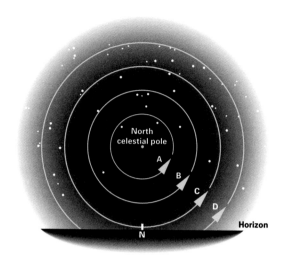

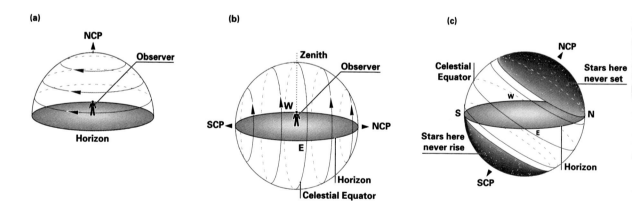

Circumpolar stars: at different latitudes (above)

a At the north (or south) pole, all stars in the visible hemisphere of sky are circumpolar – they move in circles round the celestial pole parallel to the horizon and remain at all times at the same altitude above the horizon. Stars in the other hemisphere of the celestial sphere never rise.

b At the equator, no stars are circumpolar. The celestial equator passes vertically overhead and the celestial poles are on the horizon. All stars rise and set and every part of the celestial sphere can be seen at some time or other.

c Elsewhere, some stars rise and set, some are circumpolar (never set) and others never rise.

Although you could only see half of the celestial sphere at any particular instant (the rest being hidden below the horizon), all of the stars would rise and set at some time or other. If you were to travel southwards from the north pole the north celestial pole would sink lower and lower. As you crossed the equator, the north celestial pole would sink below the northern horizon and the south celestial pole would begin to rise above the southern horizon. The further south you went, the higher it would rise until eventually the south celestial pole would be directly overhead.

Great Britain is a little more than half-way from the equator to the north pole, and the celestial pole is a little more than half-way up from the horizon to the zenith (the point vertically overhead). The altitude of the pole is always equal to your latitude on the Earth's surface.

Stars that are sufficiently close to the celestial pole trace out small circles around it and never dip below the horizon. Stars which remain at all times above your horizon are called circumpolar stars.

Stars which are too near the other celestial pole trace out small circles round that pole and can never be seen because they cannot rise above your horizon (from latitude 52°N, no star further south than declination −38° can ever be seen). Apart from these, and the circumpolar stars, all stars rise and set as the Earth turns round.

The Colours of the Stars

A casual glance at the starry night sky would suggest that all stars are tiny points of white light, but a closer inspection will show that some, at least, have different colours. Betelgeuse and Aldebaran, for example, look reddish, Capella, in Auriga, is a slightly yellowish star, Sirius and Vega appear white, and so on. Binoculars, which gather more light than the unaided human eye, show up the colours more clearly, and telescopes can make the colours even more apparent, particularly when stars of contrasting colours are seen, close together, in the same field of view (the 'field of view' is the region of sky visible at one time through a telescope or binoculars).

Light Pollution

For those who live in cities, towns or even small villages there is often so much artificial lighting around that the sky is flooded with light and only the very brightest stars can be seen; indeed, sometimes it is so bad that no stars at all can be seen. Even out in the countryside, the sky-glow from distant towns and cities, and from motorway lighting, can contribute substantially to sky brightness.

Thanks to campaigning by astronomers and others, more and more people are becoming aware of the menace of light pollution and of how so many of us are being deprived of the experience of seeing the majesty of the star-spangled sky. The amount of artificial lighting at night, wastefully directed upwards to the sky, is dramatically revealed in images of Earth taken from space by satellites. Obviously, lighting at night time is vital for a great many reasons but, as many lighting engineers appreciate, there are ways in which lighting can be made more efficient, and therefore more economical to run, by ensuring that the light is directed downwards, where it is needed, rather than upwards, where it is wasted and serves only to cast an unwanted glow over the sky. The effects of man-made lighting can never be eliminated, but it can be reduced by careful planning and consultation. Improvements are already happening, but more needs to be done to help preserve the legacy of the night sky.

How Far Are the Stars?

The distances to the nearer stars are measured by using the principle of parallax, the principle used to measure the distances of the planets described in Chapter 4.

The stars are much more distant than the planets. Because even the nearest star is 250,000 times further away than the Sun, there is no way that observations made from different locations on the Earth's surface will show a measurable shift in the position of a star! Instead, astronomers make use of the diameter of the Earth's orbit. If two measurements of the position of a nearby star are made at intervals of six months, when the Earth is on opposite sides of its orbit, those two measurements will have been made from locations separated by 300 million kilometres (186 million miles). With this long 'baseline' the chance of detecting a slight shift in the apparent position of a nearby star relative to the background of much more distant ones is greatly improved.

Even so, there is no star (apart from the Sun) sufficiently near for its parallax, its small shift in position, to be as large as one second of angular measurement. One second of angle, or 'second of arc', often denoted by 'arcsec', is $\frac{1}{60}$ of $\frac{1}{60}$ (i.e. $\frac{1}{3600}$) of a degree. The nearest star is Proxima Centauri,

Constellation photography

*A basic single-lens reflex (SLR)
camera mounted on a ridgid
tripod is ideal for this,
but almost any camera capable
of taking a prolonged time
exposure may be used.
Colour transparency or print
films of speeds between 100
and 400 ISO are suitable but
transparency films give better
results. High speed films can
record fainter stars in shorter
exposures. An exposure of
20–30 seconds should record a
good image. Because of the
Earth's rotation, exposures of
longer than about 30 seconds
will result in the stars moving
enough to appear as short
trails rather than round dots.
Point the camera towards the
Pole Star and leave it
exposing for 5 to 10 minutes
(longer if it's quite dark).
The result will show stars
with curved tails centred on the
celestial pole – a dramatic
demonstration of the Earth's
rotation.*

a dim red star which is much too faint to be seen with the naked eye, and which lies in the southern-hemisphere constellation of Centaurus (the Centaur). The parallax of Proxima Centauri is just 0.76 arcsec, an angle which is less than $\frac{1}{2000}$ of the apparent size of the Moon in the sky.

This tiny parallax implies that Proxima Centauri is at a distance of about 40 million million kilometres (25 million million miles). Distances like these are so vast that they are hard to comprehend but a useful way of visualizing them is to think of how long it would take for a ray of light, or a radio wave, to traverse these distances.

Light, and radio waves, travel at a speed of 300,000 kilometres (186,000 miles) per second. At this speed, light takes just over one second to reach us from the Moon, just over 8 minutes to arrive from the Sun, about 5 hours to reach Earth from Pluto, but about 4.3 years to arrive from Proxima Centauri. The distance travelled by light in one year, about 9.5 million million kilometres (5.9 million million miles), defines a unit of measurement called the light year. Proxima Centauri, then, is at a distance of 4.3 light years.

The stars that we see in the night sky lie at very different distances, and although the stars that make up the constellation patterns may appear quite close together in the sky, they can be at very different distances from us; they appear close together because they happen to lie in roughly the same direction when viewed from the Earth. In the constellation of Orion, for example, Betelgeuse is about 300 light years away, Rigel 900 or so and Mintaka, at the north-western end of Orion's Belt, is about 2300 light years distant from us. In fact, some of the stars in Orion are further from each other than we are from them.

The Stars Themselves

Proxima Centauri is $\frac{1}{10}$ of a light year nearer the Earth than the brilliant naked-eye star, Alpha Centauri. Although they lie at almost exactly the same distance, they have very different brightnesses; Alpha is the third-brightest star in the sky, but Proxima is about 100 times fainter than the faintest naked-eye star. This implies that the real luminosities of stars – the total amount of light that they actually pour out into space – must differ enormously. In fact, Alpha is similar in luminosity to our own Sun but Proxima emits less than $\frac{1}{10,000}$ of Alpha's light. Alpha Centauri appears as bright as it does mainly because it is so near to us, compared to other stars. Some stars are much more brilliant than our Sun. Betelgeuse, for example, is about 20,000 times as luminous as the Sun and Rigel shines with more than 50,000 Sun-power.

The colours of the stars indicate their different temperatures. Although we tend to think of red as a 'warm' colour and blue as a 'cold' colour, in fact, so far as stars are concerned, it is the other way round. Red stars like Betelgeuse are relatively cool, with surface temperatures of about 3000° Celsius. Yellowish stars, like Alpha Centauri, Capella or our own Sun, have temperatures of around 6000°C, whitish stars like Sirius or Vega are around 10,000°C, blue-white stars like Rigel have temperatures of around 20,000°C and the hottest blue stars have temperatures of well over 30,000°C.

The stars also differ enormously in size. At one end of the scale there are huge, cool red giants and supergiants which are vastly larger than our Sun. For example, if Betelgeuse were placed where the Sun is, then the orbits of the planets out to and including Mars would be contained inside its vast globe. At the other end of the scale, there are tiny stars, called white dwarfs, which are no larger than the Earth. There are also amazing compressed stars, called neutron stars, which are only about 10 kilometres (6 miles) in diameter, comparable in size with a terrestrial city. These compact stars are remarkably dense. A teaspoonful of white dwarf material, placed on the bathroom scales, would weigh more than a tonne, while a teaspoonful of neutron-star material would weigh a billion tonnes!

Birth, Life and Death of the Stars

Between the stars there are huge, tenuous clouds of gas, composed mainly of the lightest element, hydrogen, and the second-lightest element, helium. If a cloud, or part of a cloud, is sufficiently dense, it will begin to fall together under the influence of its own gravity. As the gas falls inwards and is squeezed to higher and higher densities, it becomes hotter and hotter until, eventually, the centre of the contracting cloud becomes so hot that nuclear reactions begin to take place. When this happens, the newly-forming star stops shrinking, and continues to shine by pouring out into space the vast amounts of energy produced by the nuclear reactions taking place deep down in its central core.

These reactions turn hydrogen into helium and convert matter into energy. Inside the Sun, for example, more than 600 million tonnes of hydrogen is converted into helium and about 4 million tonnes of matter is turned into energy every second. Although eventually the Sun will run out of 'fuel' there is no cause for alarm. The Sun is just under 5 billion years old, and astronomers believe it has enough fuel to keep it going for at least another 5 billion years.

The Vela supernova remnant

This is a shell of fine luminous gas filaments located at a distance of some 1500 light years in the southern-hemisphere constellation of Vela. Near its centre is a rapidly-spinning neutron star – the collapsed core of a star that exploded some 12 000 years ago to produce the nebula that we see today.

The Sun is a middle-aged star. Some are older, others are younger. The stars that make up the Pleiades cluster, in the constellation of Taurus, are relative newcomers. They were formed just 40 or 50 million years ago and could not have been seen by the dinosaurs because they were not born until after the dinosaurs died out. The constellation of Orion contains the best-known of all stellar nurseries – the Orion Nebula. A nebula is a glowing cloud of gas that is lit up by extremely hot young stars embedded within it. Some way below Orion's Belt, in the group of faint stars that make up the 'sword' of Orion, is a faint little misty patch of light that can be glimpsed by the naked eye in good conditions, and which is easily seen with binoculars or small telescopes. This patch of light is a huge cloud of gas, more than 20 light years across and some 1600 light years distant, that is lit up by a compact group of four high-temperature stars called the Trapezium. These stars are thought to have been born just a few tens of thousands of years ago.

Other stars, such as Betelgeuse, are already in old age, approaching the ends of their lives.

When the Sun is nearing the end of its life, some 5 billion years hence, it will swell up to become a red giant. When this happens, Mercury, and possibly even Venus, will be engulfed within its expanding globe. The Earth's oceans will boil and the atmosphere will be driven off into space. Then, after a few tens of millions of years, the Sun will lose most of its outer gas into space, and what remains will shrink into a compact white dwarf that eventually, after many billions of years, will cool down and fade from view.

More massive stars lead more spectacular lives. The more massive the star, the more luminous it becomes. A star 30 times as massive as the Sun will shine as brilliantly as a hundred thousand suns, but it will use up its reserves of fuel very quickly indeed. It will consume all the hydrogen in its core within a few million years. Its core will then shrink and become hotter, and its outer parts will expand to form a distended red supergiant. As the core shrinks its temperature will rise and new reactions will begin. The first one will turn helium into carbon, and release sufficient energy to keep the star shining for another few hundred thousand years or so. When all the helium has been turned into carbon, further reactions will take place, 'burning' carbon, then neon and oxygen, then finally turning silicon into iron. Each consecutive reaction produces heavier and heavier elements, but the available fuel at each stage is consumed ever more rapidly. Carbon burning lasts for a few thousand years, but silicon burning may last for only a few days!

When the core has turned into iron, the star has reached the end of the road. There is no fuel left for the star to burn. The core will collapse on itself at an astonishing rate, taking only seconds to shrink down to the size of a city. As the core collapses, and the outer parts of the star start to fall in on top of it, so much energy is released that the outer parts rebound and are blasted outwards in a catastrophic explosion that is called a supernova. A supernova can become as luminous as a billion suns.

The last supernova seen to take place in the Milky Way galaxy was observed by Kepler in 1604. On average, a large galaxy should have several supernovae per century, so one is long overdue in ours. The brightest supernova to be seen since then, was observed to flare up on 23 February 1987. Known as SN1987a, it took place not in the Milky Way but in our nearest neighbour galaxy, the Large Magellanic Cloud. Although the supernova was first seen in 1987, the explosion actually took place 170,000 years before that. It took all that time for light from the blast to travel across the vast gulf of space that separates us from the Large Magellanic Cloud. Despite its great distance, however, SN1987a was clearly visible to the naked eye.

The energy involved in these catastrophic explosions is sufficient to generate all the different chemical elements including nickel, copper, tin, silver and real 'heavyweights' like uranium. The debris from such explosions is scattered forth and mingles with the remaining interstellar gas clouds, contaminating the original hydrogen and helium of which these clouds are composed. The stars which eventually form from these clouds contain a larger proportion of heavier elements than the generations of stars that formed billions of years previously.

The Solar System was formed some 5 billion years ago from a cloud of this kind. As the cloud contracted under the pull of its own gravity, it began to spin ever more rapidly and flattened into a disc-like shape. The central part became the Sun while in the surrounding disc small solid particles condensed from the gas and began to stick together to make larger lumps. The larger lumps collided to form still larger bodies until, eventually, most of these bodies had accumulated into the planets that we know today. The heavy elements that make the rocks and metals of planet Earth, and many of the atoms of which we ourselves are composed, were all forged in previous generations of stars that exploded as supernovae before the Sun and Earth were born. The Earth consists of the debris of old dead stars, and so does its teeming variety of life-forms. We are all composed of a little 'stardust'. ■

Index

Numbers in *italics* refer to illustrations

Picture Credits
*Bridgeman Art Library 14; British
Library 95; City of Bristol 104;
English Heritage 27; Jennifer Fry
38; Galaxy 63; National Maritime
Museum Picture Library,
Greenwich 88; Royal Observatory
Edinburgh/AATB 123; Science
Photo Library 7, 22(both), 53, 91
with Fred Espenak/SPL 107;
Simon Fraser/SPL 43; Tony
Hallas/SPL 114; NASA/SPL 47;
National Snow and Ice Data
Center/SPL 118; Ronald
Royer/SPL 65; John Sanford/SPL
71; SERC Royal Greenwich
Observatory at Cambridge 88;
Zefa 31.*